MORAL CONDUCT

Swami Vivekananda

Advaita Ashrama
(PUBLICATION DEPARTMENT)
5 DEHI ENTALLY ROAD • KOLKATA 700 014

Published by
Swami Bodhasarananda
Adhyaksha, Advaita Ashrama
Mayavati, Champawat, Uttarakhand, Himalayas
from its Publication Department, Kolkata
Email: *mail@advaitaashrama.org*
Website: *www.advaitaashrama.org*

© *All Rights Reserved*
First Edition, November 2001
Third Reprint, September 2012
3M3C

ISBN 978-81-7505-220-8

Printed in India at
Trio Process
Kolkata 700 014

CONTENTS

Publisher's Preface	5
•Ethics and Morality:	
The Real Basis of Life	9
•Love and Renunciation:	
The Motive Power of the Universe	10
•The Philosophic Background	14
•The Rationale of Ethics	21
•Self-abnegation: The Basis of Moral Life	29
•Morality—Not an End in Itself:	
Freedom Its Goal	37
•Morality: Its Relative Aspects	41
•Morality: Its Absolute Standard	45
•Utility of Morality and Ethics	47
•Ethics: The Way and the Method	50
•Action and Its Effect on Character	57
•Ethical Principles and Practical Life	71
•The Ethical Idealism of Buddha	82

- Essential Moral Virtues:
    - Mercy and Self-sacrifice — 89
    - Service — 92
    - Duty — 95
    - Chastity — 100
    - Non-injury — 100
    - Attention to Means — 101
- Some Moral Precepts and Exhortations to Our Youths — 103
- References — 118

PUBLISHER'S PREFACE

Erosion of universal values such as truth, moral integrity, sympathy, service and the like, has become a cause of concern to the well-wishers of society all over the world. The values generally associated with religions and with prevailing religious norms of life, usually went by the name of virtues and moral principles in the early and medieval centuries. They were preached and propagated on the authority of holy scriptures and the words of the holy men. And people used to accept them in naive faith without questioning their authority or their necessity. But in the modern days of science and critical enquiry, such virtues and principles are considered as trivial by people until their veracity and usefulness are rationally explained to them. They cannot be accepted by modern minds unless what is truly universal, beneficial, and reasonable in them are shown, separated from that which is wholly sectarian or dogmatic—like the grains separated from the chaff.

Highly inspiring and illuminating thoughts on universal ethics and moral conduct are interwoven, as it were, in the very fabric of *The Complete Works of Swami*

Vivekananda published by us. The present book, *Universal Ethics and Moral Conduct*, is a compilation of such representative ideas of the great Swamiji on this subject and have been culled from his *Complete Works*. About the genesis of this compilation, a few lines from the Foreword by Mr. H. Narasimhaiah, the then Vice-Chancellor of the Bangalore University, to the 1974 edition of this book are worth quoting here. He wrote: "There is a general feeling that the present pattern of education in our country is incomplete and is not capable of improving the code of conduct of the student. Even the best of curriculum will not be conducive to the development of the human personality. Hence, many educationalists and thinkers have been fervently pleading for the inclusion of moral education as a part of regular study in schools and colleges. But we know that this is a sensitive subject consequent on our country being the home of many religions, castes, and sub-castes. Therefore, great care is to be bestowed on the preparation of a syllabus on moral and spiritual education which should be acceptable to people of all denominations. Sri Sri Prakasa Committee which was set up by the Government of India for this purpose has made valuable recommendations in this behalf. Based on these recommendations, the Ministry of Education, Government of India, requested Swami Ranganathananda to prepare a book containing universal spiritual values. Accordingly Swami Ranganathanandaji [currently the President of the Ramakrishna Math and Ramakrishna Mission], who knows the needs of the country and who has his fingers on the pulse of the youth, compiled this book from the extensive writings of Swami Vivekananda, a great patriot-monk of our country."

This book was first published by the Ministry of Education, Government of India, in 1965, then by the Bangalore University in 1974, and last by the Ramakrishna Math, Domalguda, Hyderabad, in 1979. It is indeed a source of basic ideas on value education. In publishing its present edition we earnestly hope that educationists, teachers, and students will profit as much from it now as they did when it was first brought out.

Kolkata   Publisher
24 August 2001

Ethics and Morality
The Real Basis of Life

THE BASIS OF ALL SYSTEMS, social or political, rests upon the goodness of men. No nation is great or good because Parliament enacts this or that, but because its men are great and good....People often work for the same ends but fail to recognise the fact. One must admit that law, government, politics are phases not final in any way. There is a goal beyond them where law is not needed....All great Masters teach the same thing. Christ saw that the basis is not law, that morality and purity are the only strength.[1]

Love and Renunciation
The Motive Power of the Universe

WHAT IS THE WATCHWORD of all ethical codes? "Not I, but thou", and this "I" is the outcome of the Infinite behind, trying to manifest Itself on the outside world. This little "I" is the result, and it will have to go back and join the Infinite, its own nature. Every time you say, "Not I, my brother, but thou", you are trying to go back, and every time you say "I, and not thou", you take the false step of trying to manifest the Infinite through the sense-world. That brings struggles and evils into the world, but after a time renunciation must come, eternal renunciation. The little "I" is dead and gone. Why care so much for this little life? All these vain desires of living and enjoying this life, here or in some other place, bring death.

We have been degraded down to the animal, and are now going up, to emerge out of this bondage. But we shall never be able entirely to manifest the Infinite here. We shall struggle hard, but there will come a time when we shall find that it is impossible to be perfect here, while we are bound by the senses. And then the march back to our original state of Infinity will be sounded.

This is renunciation. We shall have to get out of the difficulty by reversing the process by which we got in, and then morality and charity will begin.[1]

The watchword of all well-being, of all moral good is not "I" but "thou". Who cares whether there is a heaven or a hell, who cares if there is a soul or not, who cares if there is an unchangeable or not? Here is the world, and it is full of misery. Go out into it as Buddha did, and struggle to lessen it or die in the attempt. Forget yourselves; this is the first lesson to be learnt, whether you are a theist or an atheist, whether you are an agnostic or a Vedantist, a Christian or a Mohammedan. The one lesson obvious to all is the destruction of the little self and the building up of the real Self.

Two forces have been working side by side in parallel lines. The one says "I", the other says "not I". Their manifestation is not only in man but in animals, not only in animals but in the smallest worms. The tigress that plunges her fangs into the warm blood of a human being would give up her own life to protect her young. The most depraved man who thinks nothing of taking the lives of his brother men will, perhaps, sacrifice himself without any hesitation to save his starving wife and children. Thus throughout creation these two forces are working side by side; where you find the one, you find the other too. The one is selfishness, the other is unselfishness. The one is acquisition, the other is renunciation. The one takes, the other gives. From the lowest to the highest, the whole universe is the playground of these two forces. It does not require any demonstration; it is obvious to all.

What right has any section of the community to base the whole work and evolution of the universe upon one of these two factors alone, upon competition and struggle? What right has it to base the whole working of the universe upon passion and fight, upon competition and struggle? That these exist we do not deny; but what right has anyone to deny the working of the other force? Can any man deny that love, this "not I", this renunciation is the only positive power in the universe? The other is only the misguided employment of the power of love; the power of love brings competition, the real genesis of competition is in love. The real genesis of evil is in unselfishness. The creator of evil is good, and the end is also good. It is only misdirection of the power of good. A man who murders another is, perhaps, moved to do so by the love of his own child. His love has become limited to that one little baby, to the exclusion of the millions of other human beings in the universe. Yet, limited or unlimited, it is the same love.

Thus the motive power of the whole universe, in whatever way it manifests itself, is that one wonderful thing, unselfishness, renunciation, love, the real, the only living force in existence.[2]

The Philosophic Background

MY IDEA IS TO SHOW that the highest ideal of morality and unselfishness goes hand in hand with the highest metaphysical conception, and that you need not lower your conception to get ethics and morality, but, on the other hand, to reach a real basis of morality and ethics you must have the highest philosophical and scientific conceptions. Human knowledge is not antagonistic to human well-being. On the contrary, it is knowledge alone that will save us in every department of life—in knowledge is worship. The more we know the better for us.[1]

Man is like an infinite spring, coiled up in a small box, and that spring is trying to unfold itself; and all the social phenomena that we see are the result of this trying to unfold. All the competitions and struggles and evils that we see around us are neither

The Philosophic Background

the causes of these unfoldments, nor the effects. As one of our great philosophers says—in the case of the irrigation of a field, the tank is somewhere up on a higher level, and the water is trying to rush into the field, and is barred by a gate. But as soon as the gate is opened, the water rushes in by its own nature; and if there is dust and dirt in the way, the water rolls over them. But dust and dirt are neither the result nor the cause of this unfolding of the divine nature of man. They are coexistent circumstances, and, therefore, can be remedied.

Now, this idea, claims the Vedanta, is to be found in all religions, whether in India or outside of it; only, in some of them the idea is expressed through mythology, and in others, through symbology. The Vedanta claims that there has not been one religious inspiration, one manifestation of the divine man, however great, but it has been the expression of that infinite oneness in human nature; and all that we call ethics and morality and doing good to others is also but the manifestation of this oneness. There are moments when every man feels that he is one with the universe, and he rushes forth to express it, whether he knows it or not. This expression of oneness is what we call love and sympathy, and it is the basis of all our ethics and morality. This is summed up in the Vedanta philosophy by the celebrated aphorism, *Tat Tvam Asi*, "Thou art That".

To every man, this is taught: Thou art one with this Universal Being, and, as such, every soul that exists is your soul; and every body that exists is your body; and in hurting anyone, you hurt yourself, in loving anyone, you love yourself. As soon as a current of hatred is thrown outside, whomsoever else it hurts, it also hurts yourself; and if love comes out from you, it is bound to come back to you. For I am the universe; this universe is my body. I am the Infinite, only I am not conscious of it now; but I am struggling to get this consciousness of the Infinite, and perfection will be reached when full consciousness of this Infinite comes.[2]

Two forces seem to be working throughout nature. One of these is constantly differentiating, and the other is as constantly unifying; the one making more and more for separate individuals, the other, as it were, bringing the individuals into a mass, bringing out sameness in the midst of all this differentiation. It seems that the action of these two forces enters into every department of nature and of human life. On the physical plane, we always find the two forces most distinctly at work, separating the individuals, making them more and more distinct from other individuals, and again making them into species and classes, and bringing out similarities of expressions and form. The same holds good as regards the social life of man. Since the time when society began, these two forces have been at work, differentiating and unifying. Their action appears in various forms, and is called by various names, in different places, and at different times. But the essence is present in all—one making for differentiation, and the other for sameness; the one making for caste, and the other breaking it down; one making for classes and privileges, and the other destroying them. The whole universe seems to be the battleground of these two forces. On the one hand, it is urged, that though this unifying process exists, we ought to resist it with all our might, because it leads towards death, that perfect unity is perfect annihilation, and that when the differentiating process that is at work in this universe ceases, the universe comes to an end... On the other hand, the idea of oneness has had its advocates throughout all times. From the days of the Upanishads, the Buddhas, and Christs, and all other great preachers of religion, down to our present day, in the new political aspirations, and in the claims of the oppressed and the downtrodden, and of all those who find themselves bereft of privileges—comes out the one assertion of this unity and sameness...

Applied to metaphysics, this question also assumes another form... One side wants us to keep to the phenomenal, to all this variation, and points out, with great show of argument, that variation has to remain, for when that stops, everything is gone. What we mean by life has been caused by variation. The other side, at the same time, valiantly points to unity... The one side, the Greek side, which is represented by modern Europe, insisted upon the knowledge of man; the Indian side, mostly represented by the old religions of the world, insisted upon the knowledge of God. To us, at the present time, perhaps, has been given the privilege of standing aside from both these aspects, and taking an impartial view of the whole.

Ethics is unity; its basis is love. It will not look at this variation. The one aim of ethics is this unity, this sameness. The highest ethical codes that mankind has discovered up to the present time know no variation; they have no time to stop to look into it; their one end is to make for that sameness...

[But] this is a fact that variation exists, and so it must, if life is to be....A state of things, where all variation has died down, giving place to a uniform, dead homogeneity, is impossible so long as life lasts. Nor is it desirable. At the same time, there is the other side of the fact, viz. that this unity already exists. That

THE PHILOSOPHIC BACKGROUND 19

is the peculiar claim—not that this unity has to be made, but that it already exists, and that you could not perceive the variety at all, without it. God is not to be made, but He already exists. This has been the claim of all religions. Whenever one has perceived the finite, he has also perceived the Infinite… For we are bound by the logical necessity of our minds to confess that it is there, else, the perception of the finite would not be… Therefore, the absolute sameness of conditions, if that be the aim of ethics, appears to be impossible. That all men should be the same, could never be, however we might try… At the same time ring in our ears the wonderful words of morality proclaimed by various teachers: "Thus, seeing the same God equally present in all, the sage does not injure Self by the Self, and thus reaches the highest goal. Even in this life they have conquered relative existence whose minds are firmly fixed on this sameness; for God is pure, and God is the same to all. Therefore such are said to be living in God." We cannot deny that this is the real idea; yet at the same time comes the difficulty that the sameness as regards external forms and position can never be attained…

The work of ethics has been, and will be in the future not the destruction of variation and the establishment of sameness in the external world—which is impossible, for it would bring death and annihilation—but to recognise the unity in spite of all these variations, to recognise the God within in spite of everything that frightens us, to recognise that infinite strength as the property of everyone in spite of all apparent weakness, and to recognise the eternal, infinite, essential purity of the soul in spite of everything to the contrary that appears on the surface.[3]

The Rationale of Ethics

THE RATIONAL WEST IS earnestly bent upon seeking out the rationality, the *raison d'être* of all its philosophy and its ethics; and you all know well that ethics cannot be derived from the mere sanction of any personage, however great and divine he may have been. Such an explanation of the authority of ethics appeals no more to the highest of the world's thinkers; they want something more than human sanction for ethical and moral codes to be binding, they want some eternal principle of truth as the sanction of ethics.

And where is that eternal sanction to be found except in the only Infinite Reality that exists in you and in me and in all, in the Self, in the Soul? The infinite oneness of the Soul is the eternal sanction of all morality, that you and I are not only brothers—every literature voicing man's struggle towards freedom has preached that for you—but that you and I are really one…

This oneness is the rationale of all ethics and all spirituality. Europe wants it today just as much as our downtrodden masses do, and this great principle is even now unconsciously forming the basis of all the latest political and social aspirations that are coming up in England, in Germany, in France, and in America.[1]

The process that is going on in the cosmos on a large scale, is the same as that going on in the microcosm on a smaller scale. Just as this universe has its existence in separation, in distinction, and all the while is rushing towards unity, non-separation, so in our little worlds, each soul is born, as it were, cut off from the rest of the world. The more ignorant, the more unenlightened the soul, the more it thinks that it is separate from the rest of the universe. The more ignorant the person, the more he thinks he will die or will be born, and so forth—ideas that are an expression of this separateness. But we find that, as knowledge comes, man grows, morality is evolved, and the idea of non-separateness begins. Whether men understand it or not, they are impelled by that power behind to become unselfish. That is the foundation of all morality. It is the quintessence of all ethics preached in any language, or in any religion, or by any prophet in the world. "Be thou unselfish", "Not 'I', but 'thou'"—that is the background of all ethical codes. And what is meant by this is the recognition of non-individuality—that you are a part of me, and I of you; the recognition, that in hurting you I hurt myself, and in helping you, I help myself; the recognition that there cannot possibly be death for me when you live. When one worm lives in this universe, how can I die? For my life is in the life of that worm. At the same time it will teach us that we cannot leave one of our fellow-beings without helping him, that in his good consists my good.[2]

In the lowest worm, as well as in the highest human being, the same divine nature is present. The worm form is the lower form in which the divinity has been more overshadowed by *Maya*; that is the highest form in which it has been least overshadowed. Behind everything the same divinity is existing, and out of this comes the basis of morality. Do not injure another. Love everyone as your own self, because the whole universe is one. In injuring another, I am injuring myself; in loving another, I am loving myself. From this also springs that principle of Advaita morality which has been summed up in one word—self-abnegation. The Advaitist says, this little personalised self is the cause of all my misery. This individualised self, which makes me different from all other beings brings hatred and jealousy and misery, struggle, and all other evils. And when this idea has been got rid of, all struggle will cease, all misery vanish. So this is to be given up. We must always hold ourselves ready, even to give up our lives for the lowest beings. When a man has become ready even to give up his life for a little insect, he has reached the perfection....[3]

He alone lives whose life is in the whole universe, and the more we concentrate our lives on limited things, the faster we go towards death. Those moments alone we live when our lives are in the universe, in others; and living this little life is death, simply death, and that is why the fear of death comes....Says an old Sanskrit philosopher: It is only the Spirit that is the individual, because it is infinite....The apparent man is merely a struggle to express, to manifest this individuality which is beyond; and evolution is not in the Spirit. These changes which are going on—the wicked becoming good, the animal becoming man, take them in whatever way you like—are not in the Spirit. They are evolution of nature and manifestation of Spirit.

Suppose there is a screen hiding you from me, in which there is a small hole through which I can see some of the faces before me, just a few faces. Now suppose the hole begins to grow larger and larger, and as it does so, more and more of the scene before me reveals itself, and when at last the whole screen has disappeared, I stand face to face with you all.... Every good thought that you think or act upon is simply tearing the veil, as it were; and the purity, the Infinity, the God behind, manifests Itself more and more...

It is the real nature of every man, and he is struggling to express it in various ways; otherwise, why are there so many ethical codes? Where is the explanation of all ethics? One idea stands out as the centre of all ethical systems, expressed in various forms, namely, doing good to others. The guiding motive of mankind should be charity towards men, charity towards all animals. But these are all various expressions of that eternal truth that, "I am the universe; this universe is one." Or else, where is the reason? Why should I do good to my fellowmen? Why should I do good to others? What compels me? It is sympathy, the feeling of sameness everywhere. The hardest hearts feel sympathy for other beings sometimes. Even the man who gets frightened if he is told that this assumed individuality is really a delusion, that it is ignoble to try to cling to this apparent individuality, that very man will tell you that extreme self-abnegation is the centre of all morality. And what is perfect self-abnegation? It means the abnegation of this apparent self, the abnegation of all selfishness. This idea of "me and mine"—*Ahamkāra* and *Mamatā*—is the result of past superstition, and the more this present self passes away, the more the real Self becomes manifest. This is true self-abnegation, the centre, the basis, the gist of all moral teaching; and whether man knows it or not, the whole world is slowly going towards it, practising it more or less. Only, the vast majority of mankind are doing it unconsciously. Let them do it consciously. Let them make the sacrifice, knowing that this "me and mine" is not the real Self, but only a limitation. But one glimpse of that infinite reality which is behind—but one spark of that infinite fire that is the All—represents the present man; the Infinite is his true nature.[4]

There is a little circle within which human reason must move. It cannot go beyond. Every attempt to go beyond is impossible, yet it is beyond this circle of reason that there lies all that humanity holds most dear....All our ethical theories, all our moral attitudes, all that is good and great in human nature, have been moulded upon answers that have come from beyond the circle....If life is only a short play, if the universe is only a "fortuitous combination of atoms," then why should I do good to another? Why should there be mercy, justice, or fellow-feeling? The best thing for this world would be to make hay while the sun shines, each man for himself. If there is no hope, why should I love my brother, and not cut his throat? If there is nothing beyond, if there is no freedom, but only rigorous dead laws, I should only try to make myself happy here. You will find people saying nowadays that they have utilitarian grounds as the basis of morality. What is this basis? Procuring the greatest amount of happiness to the greatest number. Why should I do this? Why should I not produce the greatest unhappiness to the greatest number, if that serves my purpose? How will utilitarians answer this question? How do you know what is right, or what is wrong? I am impelled by my desire for happiness, and I fulfil it, and it is in my nature; I know nothing beyond. I have these desires, and must fulfil them; why should you complain? Whence come all these truths about human life, about morality, about the immortal soul, about God, about love and sympathy, about being good, and, above all, about being unselfish?

All ethics, all human action and all human thought, hang upon this one idea of unselfishness. The whole idea of human life can be put into that one word, unselfishness. Why should we be unselfish?

Where is the necessity, the force, the power, of my being unselfish? You call yourself a rational man, a utilitarian; but if you do not show me a reason for utility, I say you are irrational. Show me the reason why I should not be selfish. To ask one to be unselfish may be good as poetry, but poetry is not reason. Show me a reason. Why shall I be unselfish, and why be good? Because Mr. and Mrs. So-and-so say so does not weigh with me. Where is the utility of my being unselfish? My utility is to be selfish if utility means the greatest amount of happiness. What is the answer? The utilitarian can never give it. The answer is that this world is only one drop in an infinite ocean, one link in an infinite chain.[5]

Self-abnegation
The Basis of Moral Life

ETHICS ALWAYS SAYS, "Not I, but thou." Its motto is, "Not self, but non-self." The vain ideas of individualism, to which man clings when he is trying to find that Infinite Power or that Infinite Pleasure through the senses, have to be given up—says the laws of ethics. You have to put *yourself* last, and others before you. The senses say, "Myself first." Ethics says, "I must hold myself last." Thus, all codes of ethics are based upon this renunciation; destruction, not construction, of the individual on the material plane. That Infinite will never find expression upon the material plane, nor is it possible or thinkable.

So, man has to give up the plane of matter and rise to other spheres to seek a deeper expression of that Infinite. In this way the various ethical laws are being moulded, but all have that one central idea, eternal self-abnegation. Perfect self-annihilation is the ideal of ethics. People are startled if they are asked not to think of their individualities. They seem so very much afraid of losing what they call their individuality. At the same time, the same men would declare the highest ideals of ethics to be right, never for a moment thinking that the scope, the goal, the idea of all ethics is the destruction, and not the building up, of the individual.

Utilitarian standards cannot explain the ethical relations of men, for, in the first place, we cannot derive any ethical laws from considerations of utility. Without the supernatural sanction as it is called, or the perception of the superconscious, as I prefer to term it, there can be no ethics. Without the struggle towards the Infinite there can be no ideal. Any system that wants to bind men down to the limits of their own societies is not able to find an explanation for the ethical laws of mankind. The Utilitarian wants us to give up the struggle after the Infinite, the reaching-out for the Super-sensuous, as impracticable and absurd, and, in the same breath, asks us to take up ethics and do good to society. Why should we do good? Doing good is a secondary consideration. We must have an ideal. Ethics itself is not the end, but

SELF-ABNEGATION

the means to the end. If the end is not there, why should we be ethical? Why should I do good to other men, and not injure them? If happiness is the goal of mankind, why should I not make myself happy and others unhappy? What prevents me? In the second place, the basis of utility is too narrow. All the current social forms and methods are derived from society as it exists, but what right has the Utilitarian to assume that society is eternal? Society did not exist ages ago, possibly will not exist ages hence. Most probably it is one of the passing stages through which we are going towards a higher evolution, and any law that is derived from society alone cannot be eternal, cannot cover the whole ground of man's nature. At best, therefore, Utilitarian theories can only work under present social conditions. Beyond that they have no value. But a morality, an ethical code, derived from religion and spirituality, has the whole of infinite man for its scope. It takes up the individual, but its relations are to the Infinite, and it takes up society also—because society is nothing but numbers of these individuals grouped together; and as it applies to the individual and *his* eternal relations, it must necessarily apply to the whole of society, in whatever condition it may be at any given time.[1]

First, we have to bear in mind that we are all debtors to the world and the world does not owe us anything. It is a great privilege for all of us to be allowed to do anything for the world. In helping the world we really help ourselves. The second point is that there is a God in this universe. It is not true that this universe is drifting and stands in need of help from you and me. God is ever present therein, He is undying and eternally active and infinitely watchful. When the whole universe sleeps, He sleeps not; He is working incessantly; all the changes and manifestations of the world are His. Thirdly, we ought not to hate anyone. This world will always continue to be a mixture of good and evil. Our duty is to sympathise with the weak and to love even the wrongdoer. The world is a grand moral gymnasium wherein we have all to take exercise so as to become stronger and stronger spiritually. Fourthly, we ought not to be fanatics of any kind, because fanaticism is opposed to love....And further, the calmer we are and the less disturbed our nerves, the more shall we love and the better will our work be.[2]

You will find various classes of men in this world. First, there are the God-men, whose self-abnegation is complete, and who do only good to others even at the sacrifice of their own lives. These are the highest of men. If there are a hundred of such in any country, that country need never despair. But they are unfortunately too few. Then there are the good men

SELF-ABNEGATION

who do good to others so long as it does not injure themselves. And there is a third class who, to do good to themselves, injure others. It is said by a Sanskrit poet that there is a fourth unnameable class of people who injure others merely for injury's sake. Just as there are at one pole of existence the highest good men, who do good for the sake of doing good, so, at the other pole, there are others who injure others just for the sake of the injury. They do not gain anything thereby, but it is their nature to do evil.

Here are two Sanskrit words. The one is *Pravritti*, which means revolving towards, and the other is *Nivritti*, which means revolving away. The "revolving towards" is what we call the world, the "I and mine"; it includes all those things which are always enriching that "me" by wealth and money and power, and name and fame, and which are of a grasping nature, always tending to accumulate everything in one centre, that centre being "myself". That is the *Pravritti*, the natural tendency of every human being; taking everything from everywhere and heaping it around one centre, that centre being man's own sweet self. When this tendency begins to break, when it is *Nivritti* or "going away from," then begins morality and religion. Both *Pravritti* and *Nivritti* are of the nature of work: the former is evil work, and the latter is good work. This *Nivritti* is the fundamental basis of all morality and all religion, and the very perfection of it is entire self-abnegation, readiness to sacrifice mind and body and everything for another being....This is the highest result of good works. Although a man has not studied a single system of philosophy, although he does not believe in any God, and never has believed, although he has not prayed even once in his whole life, if the simple power of good actions has brought him to that state where he is ready to give up his life and all else for others, he has arrived at the same point to which the religious man will come through his prayers and the philosopher through his knowledge....Here, it is not at all any question of creed, or doctrine—even men who are very much opposed to all religious ideas, when they see one of these acts of complete self-sacrifice, feel that they must revere it.[3]

Desires of materialisation, that is, being dragged down more and more to the plane of mechanical action, belong to the animal man. It is only when the desire to prevent all such bondage to the senses arises that religion dawns in the heart of man. Thus we see that the whole scope of religion is to prevent man from falling into the bondage of the senses and to help him to assert his freedom. The first effort of this power of *Nivritti* towards that end is called morality. The scope of all morality is to prevent this degradation and break this bondage. All morality can be divided into the positive and the negative elements; it says either, "Do this" or "Do not do this". When it says, "Do not", it is evident that it is a check to a certain desire which would make a man a slave. When it says, "Do", its scope is to show the way to freedom and to the breaking down of a certain degradation which has already seized the human heart.

Now this morality is only possible if there be a liberty to be attained by man.[4]

There is being, "x", which is manifesting itself as both mind and matter. Its movements in the seen are along certain fixed lines called law. As a unity, it is free; as many, it is bound by law. Still, with all this bondage, an idea of freedom is ever present, and this is *Nivritti*, or the "dragging from attachment". The materialising forces which through desire lead us to take an active part in worldly affairs are called *Pravritti*.

That action is moral which frees us from the bondage of matter and *vice versa*.[5]

It is only through the idea of the Impersonal God that you can have any system of ethics. In every nation the truth has been preached from the most ancient times—love your fellow-beings as yourselves—I mean, love human beings as yourselves. In India it has been preached, "love all beings as yourselves";

we make no distinction between men and animals. But no reason was forthcoming, no one knew why it would be good to love other beings as ourselves. And the reason, why, is there in the idea of the Impersonal God; you understand it when you learn that the whole world is one—the oneness of the universe—the solidarity of all life—that in hurting any one I am hurting myself, in loving any one I am loving myself. Hence we understand why it is that we ought not to hurt others. The reason for ethics, therefore, can only be had from this ideal of the Impersonal God.[6]

Morality—Not an End in Itself
Freedom Its Goal

MORALITY, OF COURSE, is not the goal of man, but the means through which this freedom is attained. The Vedanta says that *Yoga* is one way that makes men realise this divinity. The Vedanta says this is done by the realisation of the freedom within and that everything will give way to that. Morality and ethics will all range themselves in their proper places.[1]

Everything that we perceive around us is struggling towards freedom, from the atom to the man, from the insentient, lifeless particle of matter to the highest existence on earth, the human soul. The whole universe is in fact the result of this struggle for freedom. In all combinations, every particle is trying to go on its own way, to fly from the other particles;

but the others are holding it in check. Our earth is trying to fly away from the sun, and the moon from the earth. Everything has a tendency to infinite dispersion. All that we see in the universe has for its basis this one struggle towards freedom; it is under the impulse of this tendency that the saint prays and the robber robs. When the line of action taken is not a proper one, we call it evil; and when the manifestation of it is proper and high, we call it good. But the impulse is the same, the struggle towards freedom. The saint is oppressed with the knowledge of his condition of bondage, and he wants to get rid of it; so he worships God. The thief is oppressed with the idea that he does not possess certain things, and he tries to get rid of that want, to obtain freedom from it; so he steals. Freedom is the one goal of all nature, sentient or insentient; and consciously or unconsciously, everything is struggling towards that goal. The freedom which the saint seeks is very different from that which the robber seeks; the freedom loved by the saint leads him to the enjoyment of infinite, unspeakable bliss, while that on which the robber has set his heart only forges other bonds for his soul.

There is to be found in every religion the manifestation of this struggle towards freedom. It is the groundwork of all morality, of unselfishness, which means getting rid of the idea that men are the same as their little body. When we see a man doing good work, helping others, it means that he cannot be confined within the limited circle of "me and mine". There is no limit to this getting out of selfishness. All the great systems of ethics preach absolute unselfishness as the goal. Supposing this absolute unselfishness can be reached by a man, what becomes of him? He is no more the little Mr. So-and-so; he has acquired infinite expansion. The little personality which he had before is now lost to him for ever; he has become infinite, and the attainment of this infinite expansion is indeed the goal of all religions and of all moral and philosophical teachings. The personalist, when he hears this idea philosophically put, gets frightened. At the same time, if he preaches morality, he, after all, teaches the very same idea himself. He puts no limit to the unselfishness of man. Suppose a man becomes perfectly unselfish under the personalistic system, how are we to distinguish him from the perfected ones in other systems? He has become one with the universe and to become that is the goal of all; only the poor personalist has not the courage to follow out his own reasoning to its right conclusion. *Karma-Yoga* is the attaining through unselfish work of that freedom which is the goal of all human nature. Every selfish action, therefore, retards our reaching the goal, and every unselfish action takes us towards the goal; that is why the only definition that can be given of morality is this: *That which is selfish is immoral, and that which is unselfish is moral.*[2]

Morality
Its Relative Aspects

ONE SET OF MORAL RULES cannot be preached to all....All sectarian religions take for granted that all men are equal. This is not warranted by science. There is more difference between minds than between bodies...

Every man, in every age, in every country, is under peculiar circumstances. If the circumstances change, ideas also must change. Beef-eating was once moral. The climate was cold, and the cereals were not much known. Meat was the chief food available. So in that age and clime, beef was in a manner indispensable. But beef-eating is held to be immoral now. The one thing unchangeable is God.[1]

Human society is a graded organisation. We all know about morality, and we all know about duty, but at the same time we find that in different countries the significance of morality varies greatly. What is regarded as moral in one country may in another be considered perfectly immoral. For instance, in one country cousins may marry; in another, it is thought to be very immoral; in one, men may marry their sisters-in-law; in another, it is regarded as immoral; in one country, people may marry only once; in another, many times; and so forth. Similarly, in all other departments of morality, we find the standard varies greatly, yet we have the idea that there must be a universal standard of morality.

So it is with duty. The idea of duty varies much among different nations. In one country, if a man does not do certain things, people will say he has acted wrongly; while if he does those very things in another country, people will say that he did not act rightly; and yet we know that there must be some universal idea of duty. In the same way, one class of society thinks that certain things are among its duty, while another class thinks quite the opposite and would be horrified if it had to do those things.

Two ways are left open to us—the way of the ignorant, who thinks that there is only one way to truth and that all the rest are wrong, and the way of the wise, who admit that, according to our mental constitution or the different planes of existence in which we are, duty and morality may vary. The important thing is to know that there are gradations of duty and of morality, that the duty of one state of life, in one set of circumstances will not and cannot be that of another...

Every man should take up his own ideal and endeavour to accomplish it. That is a surer way of progress than taking up other men's ideals, which he can never hope to accomplish. For instance, we take a child and at once give him the task of walking twenty miles. Either the little one dies, or one in a thousand crawls the twenty miles, to reach the end exhausted and half-dead. That is like what we generally try to do with the world. All the men and women, in any society, are not of the same mind, capacity, or of the same power to do things; they must have different ideals, and we have no right to sneer at any ideal. Let every one do the best he can for realising his own ideal. Nor is it right that I should be judged by your standard or you by mine. The apple tree should not be judged by the standard of the oak, nor the oak by that of the apple. To judge the apple tree you must take the apple standard, and for the oak, its own standard.

Unity in variety is the plan of creation. However men and women may vary individually, there is unity in the background. The different individual characters and classes of men and women are natural variations in creation. Hence, we ought not to judge them by the same standard or put the same ideal before them. Such a course creates only an unnatural struggle, and the result is that man begins to hate himself and is hindered from becoming religious and good. Our duty is to encourage every one in his struggle to live up to his own highest ideal, and strive at the same time to make the ideal as near as possible to the truth.

In the Hindu system of morality we find that this fact has been recognised from very ancient times; and in their scriptures and books on ethics different rules are laid down for the different classes of men—the householder, the *Sannyasin*, and the student.[2]

Morality
Its Absolute Standard

IF YOU COME TO DETAILS, the matter will not be seen to be quite so simple. For instance, environment often makes the details different as I have already mentioned. The same action under one set of circumstances may be unselfish, and under another set quite selfish. So we can give only a general definition, and leave the details to be worked out by taking into consideration the differences in time, place, and circumstances. In one country, one kind of conduct is considered moral, and in another the very same is immoral, because the circumstances differ. The goal of all nature is freedom, and freedom is to be attained only by perfect unselfishness; every thought, word, or deed that is unselfish takes us towards the goal, and, as such, is called moral. That definition, you will find, holds good in every religion and every system of ethics. In some systems of thought, morality is derived from a Superior Being—God. If you ask why a man ought to do this and not that, their answer is: "Because such is the command of God." But whatever be the source from which it is derived, their code of ethics also has the same central idea: not to think of self but to give up self. And yet some persons, in spite of this high ethical idea, are frightened at the thought of having to give up their little personalities. We may ask the man who clings to the idea of little personalities to consider the case of a person who has become perfectly unselfish, who has no thought for himself, who does no deed for himself, who speaks no word for himself, and then say where his "himself" is. That "himself" is known to him only so long as he thinks, acts, or speaks for himself. If he is only conscious of others, of the universe, and of the all, where is his "himself"? It is gone forever.[1]

Utility of Morality and Ethics

IN THESE DAYS, WE HAVE to measure everything by utility—by how many pounds, shillings, and pence it represents. What right has a person to ask that truth should be judged by the standard of utility or money? Suppose there is no utility, will it be less true? Utility is not the test of truth. Nevertheless, there is the highest utility in this. Happiness, we see, is what everyone is seeking for, but the majority seek it in things which are evanescent and not real. No happiness was ever found in the senses. There never was a person who found happiness in the senses or in the enjoyment of the senses. Happiness is only found in the Spirit. Therefore the highest utility for mankind is to find this happiness in the Spirit. The next point is that ignorance is the great mother of all misery, and the fundamental ignorance is to think that the Infinite weeps and cries....that we are little minds, that we are little bodies; it is the mother of all selfishness. As soon as I think that I am a little body, I want to preserve it, to protect it, to keep it nice, at the expense of other bodies; then you and I become separate. As soon as this idea of separation comes, it opens the door to all mischief and leads to all misery. This is the utility that if a very small fractional part of human beings living today can put aside the idea of selfishness, narrowness, and littleness, this earth will become a paradise tomorrow; but with machines and improvements of material knowledge only, it will never be. These only increase misery, as oil poured on fire increases the flame all the more. Without the knowledge of the Spirit, all material knowledge is only adding fuel to fire, only giving into the hands of selfish man one more instrument to take what belongs to others, to live upon the life of others, instead of giving up his life for them.[1]

This world is a mixture of good and evil, happiness and misery, and that to increase the one, one must of necessity increase the other. There will never be a perfectly good or bad world, because the very idea is a contradiction in terms. The great secret revealed by this analysis is that good and bad are not two cut-and-dried, separate existences. There is not

UTILITY OF MORALITY AND ETHICS 49

one thing in this world of ours which you can label as good and good alone, and there is not one thing in the universe which you can label as bad and bad alone. The very same phenomenon which is appearing to be good now, may appear to be bad tomorrow. The same thing which is producing misery in one, may produce happiness in another. The fire that burns the child, may cook a good meal for a starving man. ...What, then,...is the use of doing good work? This is a question that comes to the mind. If it is true that you cannot do good without doing evil, and whenever you try to create happiness there will always be misery, people will ask you: "What is the use of doing good?" The answer is, in the first place, that we must work for lessening misery, for that is the only way to make ourselves happy. Every one of us finds it out sooner or later in our lives. The bright ones find it out a little earlier, and the dull ones a little later. The dull ones pay very dearly for the discovery and the bright ones less dearly. In the second place, we must do our part, because that is the only way of getting out of this life of contradiction. Both the forces of good and evil will keep the universe alive for us, until we awake from our dreams and give up this building of mud pies. That lesson we shall have to learn, and it will take a long, long time to learn it.[2]

Ethics
The Way and the Method

THE GREAT ERROR IN ALL ethical systems, without exception, has been the failure of teaching the means by which man could refrain from doing evil. All the systems of ethics teach, "Do not steal." Very good; but why does a man steal? Because all stealing, robbing, and other evil actions, as a rule, have become automatic. The systematic robber, thief, liar, unjust man and woman, are all these in spite of themselves! It is really a tremendous psychological problem. We should look upon man in the most charitable light. It is not so easy to be good. What are you but mere machines until you are free? Should you be proud because you are good? Certainly not. You are good because you cannot help it. Another is bad because

ETHICS: THE WAY AND THE METHOD 51

he cannot help it. If you were in his position, who knows what you would have been. The woman in the street, or the thief in the jail, is the Christ that is being sacrificed that you may be a good man. Such is the law of balance. All the thieves and the murderers, all the unjust, the weakest, the wickedest, the devils, they are all my Christ! I owe a worship to the God Christ and to the demon Christ! That is my doctrine, I cannot help it. My salutation goes to the feet of the good, the saintly, and to the feet of the wicked and the devilish! They are all my teachers, all are my spiritual fathers, all are my Saviours. I may curse one and yet benefit by his failings; I may bless another and benefit by his good deeds. This is as true as that I stand here. I have to sneer at the woman walking in the street, because society wants it! She, my saviour, she, whose street-walking is the cause of the chastity of other women; think of that. Think, men and women, of this question in your mind. It is a truth—a bare, bold truth! As I see more of the world, see more of the men and women, this conviction grows stronger. Whom shall I blame? Whom shall I praise? Both sides of the shield must be seen.

The task before us is vast; and first and foremost, we must seek to control the vast mass of sunken thoughts which have become automatic with us. The evil deed is, no doubt, on the conscious plane; but the cause which produced the evil deed was far beyond in the realms of the unconscious, unseen, and therefore more potent....But mind you, if the power of evil is in the unconscious, so also is the power of good. We have many things stored in us as in a pocket. We have forgotten them, do not even think of them, and there are many of them, rotting, becoming positively dangerous; they come forth, the unconscious causes which kill humanity. True psychology would, therefore, try to bring them under the control of the conscious. The great task is to revive the whole man, as it were, in order to make him the complete master of himself.[1]

We hear "Be good," and "Be good," and "Be good," taught all over the world. There is hardly a child born in any country in the world, who has not been told, "Do not steal," "Do not tell a lie," but nobody tells the child how he can help doing them. Talking will not help him. Why should he not become a thief? We do not teach him how not to steal; we simply tell him, "Do not steal." Only when we teach him to control his mind do we really help him. All actions, internal and external, occur when the mind joins itself to certain centres, called the organs. Willingly or unwillingly it is drawn to join itself to the centres, and that is why people do foolish deeds and feel miserable, which, if the mind were under control, they would not do. What would be the result of controlling the mind? It then would not join itself to the centres of perception, and, naturally, feeling and willing would be under control. It is clear so far. Is it possible? It is perfectly possible. You see it in modern times; the faith-healers teach people to deny misery and pain and evil. Their philosophy is rather roundabout...the control of the centres which is established in a hypnotic patient or the patient of faith-healing, by the operator, for a time, is reprehensible, because it leads to ultimate ruin. It is not really controlling the brain centres by the power of one's own will, but is, as it were, stunning the patient's mind for a time by sudden blows which another's will delivers to it. It is not checking by means of reins and muscular strength the mad career of a fiery team, but rather by asking another to deliver heavy blows on the heads of the horses, to stun them for a time into gentleness. At each one of these processes the man operated upon loses a part of his mental energies, till at last, the mind, instead of gaining the power of perfect control, becomes a shapeless, powerless mass, and the only goal of the patient is the lunatic asylum.

Every attempt at control which is not voluntary, not with the controller's own mind, is not only disastrous, but it defeats the end. The goal of each soul is freedom, mastery—freedom from the slavery of matter and thought, mastery of external and internal nature. Instead of leading towards that, every will-current from another, in whatever form it comes, either as direct control of organs, or as forcing to control them while under a morbid condition, only rivets one link more to the already existing heavy chain of bondage of past thoughts, past superstitions. Therefore, beware how you allow yourselves to be acted upon by others. Beware how you unknowingly bring another to ruin. True, some succeed in doing good to many for a time, by giving a new trend to their propensities, but at the same time, they bring ruin to millions by the unconscious suggestions they throw around, rousing in men and women that morbid, passive, hypnotic condition which makes them almost soulless at last. Whosoever, therefore, asks any one to believe blindly, or drags people behind him by the controlling power of his superior will, does an injury to humanity, though he may not intend it.

Therefore use your own minds, control body and mind yourselves, remember that until you are a diseased person, no extraneous will can work upon you; avoid everyone, however great and good he may be, who asks you to believe blindly. All over the world there have been dancing and jumping and howling sects, who spread like infection when they begin to sing and dance and preach; they also are a sort of

ETHICS: THE WAY AND THE METHOD

hypnotists. They exercise a singular control, for the time being, over sensitive persons, alas! often, in the long run, to degenerate whole races. Ay, it is healthier for the individual or the race to remain wicked than be made apparently good by such morbid extraneous control.... Therefore, beware of everything that take away your freedom. Know that it is dangerous, and avoid it by all the means in your power.[2]

What is meant by morality? Making the subject strong by attuning it to the Absolute, so that finite nature ceases to have control over us. It is a logical conclusion of our philosophy that there must come a time when we shall have conquered all the environments, because nature is finite...

There are two components in every action, the one the subject, the other the object, and the one aim of life is to make the subject master of the object. For instance, I feel unhappy because a man scolds me. My struggle will be to make myself strong enough to conquer the environment, so that he may scold and I shall not feel. That is how we are all trying to conquer.... The little fish wants to fly from its enemies in the water. How does it do so? By evolving wings and becoming a bird. The fish did not change the water or the air; the change was in itself. Change is always subjective. All through evolution you find that the conquest of nature comes by change in the subject.

Apply this to religion and morality, and you will find that the conquest of evil comes by the change in the subjective alone.[3]

Action and Its Effect on Character

THE GOAL OF MANKIND is knowledge. That is the one ideal placed before us by Eastern philosophy. Pleasure is not the goal of man, but knowledge. Pleasure and happiness come to an end. It is a mistake to suppose that pleasure is the goal. The cause of all the miseries we have in the world is that men foolishly think pleasure to be the ideal to strive for. After a time man finds that it is not happiness, but knowledge, towards which he is going, and that both pleasure and pain are great teachers, and that he learns as much from evil as from good. As pleasure and pain pass before his soul they have upon it different pictures, and the result of these combined impressions is what is called man's "character". If you take the character of any man, it really is but the aggregate of tendencies, the sum total of the bent of his mind; you will find that misery and happiness are equal factors in the formation of that character. Good and evil have an equal share in moulding character, and in some instances misery is a greater teacher than happiness. In studying the great characters the world has produced, I dare say, in the vast majority of cases, it would be found that it was misery that taught more than happiness, it was poverty that taught more than wealth, it was blows that brought out their inner fire more than praise.

Now this knowledge, again, is inherent in man. No knowledge comes from outside; it is all inside. What we say a man "knows", should, in strict psychological language, be what he "discovers" or "unveils"; what a man "learns" is really what he "discovers", by taking the cover off his own soul, which is a mine of infinite knowledge.

We say Newton discovered gravitation. Was it sitting anywhere in a corner waiting for him? It was in his own mind; the time came and he found it out. All knowledge that the world has ever received comes from the mind; the infinite library of the universe is in your own mind. The external world is simply the suggestion, the occasion, which sets you to study your own mind, but the object of your study is always your own mind. The falling of an apple gave the suggestion to Newton, and he studied his own mind. He rearranged all the previous links of thought in his mind and discovered a new link among them, which we call the law of gravitation. It was not in the apple nor in anything in the centre of the earth.

All knowledge, therefore, secular or spiritual, is in the human mind. In many cases it is not discovered, but remains covered, and when the covering is being slowly taken off, we say, "We are learning," and the advance of knowledge is made by the advance of this process of uncovering. The man from whom this veil is being lifted is the more knowing man, the man upon whom it lies thick is ignorant, and the man from whom it has entirely gone is all-knowing, omniscient. There have been omniscient men, and, I believe, there will be yet; and that there will be myriads of them in the cycles to come. Like fire in a piece of flint, knowledge exists in the mind; suggestion is the friction which brings it out. So with all our feelings and actions—our tears and our smiles, our joys and our griefs, our weeping and our laughter, our curses and our blessings, our praises and our blames—every one of these we may find, if we calmly study our own selves, to have been brought out from within ourselves by so many blows. The result is what we are. All these blows taken together are called *Karma*—work, action. Every mental and physical blow that is given to the soul, by which, as it were, fire is struck from it, and by which its own power and knowledge are discovered, is *Karma*, this word being used in its widest sense. Thus we are all doing *Karma* all the time. I am talking to you: that is *Karma*. You are listening: that is *Karma*. We breathe: that is *Karma*. We walk: that is *Karma*. Everything we do, physical or mental, is *Karma*, and it leaves its marks on us.

There are certain works which are, as it were, the aggregate, the sum total, of a large number of smaller works. If we stand near the seashore and hear the waves dashing against the shingle, we think it is such a great noise, and yet we know that one wave is really composed of millions and millions of minute waves. Each one of these is making a noise, and yet we do not catch it; it is only when they become the big aggregate that we hear. Similarly, every pulsation of the heart is work. Certain kinds of work we feel and they become tangible to us; they are, at the same time, the aggregate of a number of small works. If you really want to judge of the character of a man, look not at his great performances. Every fool may become a hero at one time or another. Watch a man do his most common actions; those are indeed the things which will tell you the real character of a great man. Great occasions rouse even the lowest of human beings to some kind of greatness, but he alone is the really great man whose character is great always, the same wherever he be.

Karma in its effect on character is the most tremendous power that man has to deal with. Man is, as it were, a centre, and is attracting all the powers of the universe towards himself, and in this centre is fusing them all and again sending them off in a big current. Such a centre is the *real* man—the almighty, the omniscient—and he draws the whole universe towards him. Good and bad, misery and happiness, all are running towards him and clinging round him; and out of them he fashions the mighty stream of tendency called character and throws it outwards. As he has the power of drawing in anything, so has he the power of throwing it out.

All the actions that we see in the world, all the movements in human society, all the works that we have around us, are simply the display of thought, the manifestation of the will of man. Machines or instruments, cities, ships, or men-of-war, all these are simply the manifestation of the will of man; and this will is caused by character, and character is manufactured by *Karma*. As is *Karma*, so is the manifestation of the will. The men of mighty will the world has produced have all been tremendous workers—

gigantic souls, with wills powerful enough to overturn worlds, wills they got by persistent work, through ages and ages. Such a gigantic will as that of a Buddha or a Jesus could not be obtained in one life, for we know who their fathers were. It is not known that their fathers ever spoke a word for the good of mankind. Millions and millions of carpenters like Joseph had gone; millions are still living. Millions and millions of petty kings like Buddha's father had been in the world. If it was only a case of hereditary transmission, how do you account for this petty prince, who was not, perhaps, obeyed by his own servants, producing this son, whom half a world worships? How do you explain the gulf between the carpenter and his son, whom millions of human beings worship as God? It cannot be solved by the theory of heredity. The gigantic will which Buddha and Jesus threw over the world, whence did it come? Whence came this accumulation of power? It must have been there through ages and ages, continually growing bigger and bigger, until it burst on society in a Buddha or a Jesus, even rolling down to the present day.

All this is determined by Karma, work. No one can get anything unless he earns it. This is an eternal law. We may sometimes think it is not so, but in the long run we become convinced of it. A man may struggle all his life for riches; he may cheat thousands, but he finds at last that he did not deserve to become rich, and his life becomes a trouble and a nuisance to him. We may go on accumulating things for our physical enjoyment, but only what we earn is really ours. A fool may buy all the books in the world, and they will be in his library; but he will be able to read only those that he deserves to; and this deserving is produced by Karma. Our Karma determines what we deserve and what we can assimilate. We are responsible for what we are; and whatever we wish ourselves to be, we have the power to make ourselves. If what we are now has been the result of our own past actions, it certainly follows that whatever we wish to be in future can be produced by our present actions; so we have to know how to act.

You will say, "What is the use of learning how to work? Everyone works in some way or other in this world." But there is such a thing as frittering away our energies....By knowing how to work, one can obtain the greatest results. You must remember that all work is simply to bring out the power of the mind, which is already there, to wake up the soul. The power is inside every man, so is knowing; the different works are like blows to bring them out, to cause these giants to wake up.

Man works with various motives. There cannot be work without motive. Some people want to get fame, and they work for fame. Others want money, and they work for money. Others want to have power, and they work for power. Others want to get to heaven, and they work for the same....

There are some who are really the salt of the earth in every country and who work for work's sake, who do not care for name, or fame, or even to go to heaven. They work just because good will come out of it. There are others who do good to the poor and help mankind from still higher motives, because they believe in doing good and love good. The motive for name and fame seldom brings immediate results, as a rule; they come to us when we are old and have almost done with life. If a man works without any selfish motive in view, does he not gain anything? Yes, he gains the highest. Unselfishness is more paying, only people have not the patience to practise it. It is more paying from the point of view of health also. Love, truth and unselfishness are not merely moral figures of speech, but they form our highest ideal, because in them lies such a manifestation of power. In the first place, a man who can work for five days, or even for five minutes, without any selfish motive whatever, without thinking of future, of heaven, of punishment, or anything of the kind, has in him the capacity to become a powerful moral giant. It is hard to do it, but in the heart of our hearts we know its value, and the good it brings.

It is the greatest manifestation of power—this tremendous restraint; self-restraint is a manifestation of greater power than all outgoing action. A carriage with four horses may rush down a hill unrestrained, or the coachman may curb the horses. Which is the greater manifestation of power, to let them go or to hold them? A cannon-ball flying through the air goes a long distance and falls. Another is cut short in its flight by striking against a wall, and the impact generates intense heat. All outgoing energy following a selfish motive is frittered away; it will not cause power to return to you; but if restrained, it will result in development of power. This self-control will tend to produce a mighty will, a character which makes a Christ or a Buddha. Foolish men do not know this secret; they nevertheless want to rule mankind. Even a fool may rule the whole world if he works and waits. Let him wait a few years, restrain that foolish idea of governing; and when that idea is wholly gone, he will be a power in the world. The majority of us cannot see beyond a few years, just as some animals cannot see beyond a few steps. Just a little narrow circle—that is our world. We have not the patience to look beyond, and thus become immoral and wicked. This is our weakness, our powerlessness.

Even the lowest forms of work are not to be despised. Let the man, who knows no better, work for selfish ends, for name and fame; but everyone should always try to get towards higher and higher motives and to understand them. "To work we have the right, but not to the fruits thereof." Leave the fruits alone. Why care for results? If you wish to help a man, never think what that man's attitude should be towards you. If you want to do a great or a good work, do not trouble to think what the result will be.

There arises a difficult question in this ideal of work. Intense activity is necessary; we must always work. We cannot live a minute without work. What, then, becomes of rest? Here is one side of the life-struggle—work, in which we are whirled rapidly round. And here is the other—that of calm retiring renunciation: everything is peaceful around, there is very little of noise and show, only nature with her animals and flowers and mountains. Neither of them is a perfect picture. A man used to solitude, if brought in contact with the surging whirlpool of the world, will be crushed by it; just as the fish that lives in the deep sea water, as soon as it is brought to the surface, breaks into pieces, deprived of the weight of water on it that had kept it together. Can a man who has been used to the turmoil and the rush of life live at ease if he comes to a quiet place? He suffers and perchance may lose his mind. The ideal man is he who, in the midst of the greatest silence and solitude, finds the intensest activity, and in the midst of the intensest activity finds the silence and solitude of the desert. He has learnt the secret of restraint, he has controlled himself. He goes through the streets of a big city with all its traffic, and his mind is as calm as if he were in a cave, where not a sound could reach him; and he is intensely working all the time...

But we have to begin from the beginning, to take up the works as they come to us and slowly make ourselves more unselfish every day. We must do the work and find out the motive power that prompts us; and, almost without exception, in the first years, we shall find that our motives are always selfish; but gradually this selfishness will melt by persistence, till at last will come the time when we shall be able to do really unselfish work. We may all hope that some day or other, as we struggle through the paths of life, there will come a time when we shall become perfectly unselfish; and the moment we attain to that, all our powers will be concentrated, and the knowledge which is ours will be manifest.[1]

Samskāra can be translated very nearly by "inherent tendency". Using the simile of a lake for the mind, every ripple, every wave that rises in the mind, when it subsides, does not die out entirely, but leaves a mark and a future possibility of that wave coming out again. This mark, with the possibility of the wave reappearing, is what is called *Samskāra*. Every work that we do, every movement of the body, every thought that we think, leaves such an impression on the mind-stuff, and even when such impressions are not obvious on the surface, they are sufficiently strong to work beneath the surface, subconsciously. What we are every moment is determined by the sum total of these impressions on the mind. What I am just at this moment is the effect of the sum total of all the impressions of my past life. This is really what is meant by character; each man's character is determined by the sum total of these impressions. If good impressions prevail, the character becomes good; if bad, it becomes bad. If a man continuously hears bad words, thinks bad thoughts, does bad actions, his mind will be full of bad impressions; and they will influence his thought and work without his being conscious of the fact. In fact, these bad impressions are always working, and their resultant must be evil, and that man will be a bad man; he cannot help it. The sum total of these impressions in him will create the strong motive power for doing bad actions. He will be like a machine in the hands of his impressions, and they will force him to do evil. Similarly, if a man thinks good thoughts and does good works, the sum total of these impressions will be good; and they, in a similar manner, will force him to do good even in spite of himself. When a man has done so much good work and thought so many good thoughts that there is an irresistible tendency in him to do good, in spite of himself and even if he wishes to do evil, his mind, as the sum total of his tendencies, will not allow him to do so; the tendencies will turn him back; he is completely under the influence of the good tendencies. When such is the case, a man's good character is said to be established.[2]

The mind, to have non-attachment, must be clear, good, and rational.... Each action is like the pulsations quivering over the surface of the lake. The vibration dies out, and what is left? The *Samskāras*, the impressions. When a large number of these impressions are left on the mind, they coalesce and become a habit. It is said, "Habit is second nature", it is first nature also, and the whole nature of man; everything that we are is the result of habit. That gives us consolation, because, if it is only habit, we can make and unmake it at any time. The *Samskāras* are left by these vibrations passing out of our mind, each one of them leaving its result. Our character is the sum total of these marks, and according as some particular wave prevails one takes that tone. If good prevails, one becomes good; if wickedness, one becomes wicked; if joyfulness, one becomes happy. The only remedy for bad habits is counter habits; all the bad habits that have left their impressions are to be controlled by good habits. Go on doing good, thinking holy thoughts continuously; that is the only way to suppress base impressions. Never say any man is hopeless, because he only represents a character, a bundle of habits, which can be checked by new and better ones. Character is repeated habits, and repeated habits alone can reform character.[3]

Ethical Principles and Practical Life

THE DOCTRINE WHICH STANDS out luminously in every page of the *Gita* (the best commentary we have on the Vedanta philosophy) is intense activity, but in the midst of it, eternal calmness. This is the secret of work, to attain which is the goal of the Vedanta. Inactivity, as we understand it in the sense of passivity, certainly cannot be the goal. Were it so, then the walls around us would be the most intelligent; they are inactive. Clods of earth, stumps of trees, would be the greatest sages in the world; they are inactive. Nor does inactivity become activity when it is combined with passion. Real activity, which is the goal of Vedanta, is combined with eternal calmness, the calmness which cannot be ruffled, the balance of mind which is never disturbed, whatever happens. And we all know from our experience in life that that is the best attitude for work.

I have been asked many times how we can work if we do not have the passion which we generally feel for work. I also thought in that way years ago, but as I am growing older, getting more experience, I find it is not true. The less passion there is, the better we work. The calmer we are, the better for us, and the more the amount of work we can do. When we let loose our feelings, we waste so much energy, shatter our nerves, disturb our minds, and accomplish very little work. The energy which ought to have gone out as work is spent as mere feeling, which counts for nothing. It is only when the mind is very calm and collected that the whole of its energy is spent in doing good work. And if you read the lives of the great workers which the world has produced, you will find that they were wonderfully calm men. Nothing, as it were, could throw them off their balance. That is why the man who becomes angry never does a great amount of work, and the man whom nothing can make angry accomplishes so much. The man who gives way to anger, or hatred, or any other passion, cannot work; he only breaks himself to pieces, and does nothing practical. It is the calm, forgiving, equable, well-balanced mind that does the greatest amount of work.

There are two tendencies in human nature: one to harmonise the ideal with the life, and the other to elevate the life to the ideal. It is a great thing to understand this, for the former tendency is the temptation of our lives. I think that I can only do a certain class of work. Most of it, perhaps, is bad; most of it, perhaps, has a motive power of passion behind it, anger, or greed, or selfishness. Now if any man comes to preach to me a certain ideal, the first step towards which is to give up selfishness, to give up self-enjoyment, I think that is impractical. But when a man brings an ideal which can be reconciled with my selfishness, I am glad at once and jump at it. That is the ideal for me. So with practicality. What I think is practical, is to me the only practicality in the world. If I am a shopkeeper, I think shopkeeping the only practical pursuit in the world. If I am a thief, I think stealing is the best means of being practical; others are not practical. You see how we all use this word practical for things *we* like and can do. Therefore I will ask you to understand that Vedanta....does not preach an impossible ideal, however high it be...

The Vedanta teaches men to have faith in themselves first. As certain religions of the world say that a man who does not believe in a Personal God outside of himself is an atheist, so the Vedanta says, a man who does not believe in himself is an atheist. Not believing in the glory of our own soul is what the Vedanta calls atheism. To many this is, no doubt, a terrible idea; and most of us think that this ideal can never be reached; but the Vedanta insists that it can be realised by every one. There is neither man nor woman or child, nor difference of race or sex, nor anything that stands as a bar to the realisation of the ideal.

All the powers in the universe are already ours. It is we who have put our hands before our eyes and cry that it is dark. Know that there is no darkness around us. Take the hands away and there is the light which was from the beginning. Darkness never existed, weakness never existed. We who are fools cry that we are weak; we who are fools cry that we are impure....As soon as you say, "I am a little mortal being," you are saying something which is not true, you are giving the lie to yourselves, you are hypnotising yourselves into something vile and weak and wretched...

The greatest error, says the Vedanta, is to say that you are weak, that you are a sinner, a miserable creature, and that you have no power and you cannot do this and that. Every time you think in that way, you, as it were, rivet one more link in the chain that binds you down, you add one more layer of hypnotism on to your own soul. Therefore, whosoever thinks he is weak is wrong, whosoever thinks he is impure is wrong, and is throwing a bad thought into the world....This false life must go, and the real life which is always existing must manifest itself, must shine out. No man becomes purer and purer, it is a matter of greater manifestation. The veil drops away, and the native purity of the soul begins to manifest itself. Everything is ours already—infinite purity, freedom, love, and power. The actual should be reconciled to the ideal, the present life should be made to coincide with life eternal...

These are the principles of ethics, but we shall now come down lower and work out the details. We shall see how this Vedanta can be carried into our everyday life, the city life, the country life, the national life, and the home life of every nation...

The ideal of faith in ourselves is of the greatest help to us. If faith in ourselves had been more extensively taught and practised, I am sure a very large portion of the evils and miseries that we have would have vanished. Throughout the history of mankind, if any motive power has been more potent than another in the lives of all great men and women, it is that of faith in themselves. Born with the consciousness that they were to be great, they became great. Let a man go down as low as possible; there must come a time when out of sheer desperation he will take an upward curve and will learn to have faith in himself. But it is better for us that we should know it from the very first.…He is an atheist who does not believe in himself. The old religion said that he was an atheist who did not believe in God. The new religion says that he is the atheist who does not believe in himself. But it is not selfish faith.…It means faith in all, because you are all. Love for yourselves means love for all, love for animals, love for everything, for you are all one. It is the great faith which will make the world better. I am sure of that. He is the highest man who can say with truth, "I know all about myself." Do you know how much energy, how many powers, how many forces are still lurking behind that frame of yours? What scientist has known all that is in man? Millions of years have passed since man first came here, and yet but one infinitesimal part of his powers has been manifested. Therefore, you must not say that you are weak.…For behind you is the ocean of infinite power and blessedness.

Let the world resound with this ideal, and let superstitions vanish. Tell it to men who are weak and persist in telling it. You are the Pure One; awake and arise, O mighty one, this sleep does not become you. Awake and arise, it does not befit you. Think not that you are weak and miserable. Almighty, arise and awake, and manifest your own nature. It is not fitting that you think yourself a sinner. It is not fitting that you think yourself weak. Say that to the world, say it to yourselves, and see what a practical result comes, see how with an electric flash everything is manifested, how everything is changed. Tell that to mankind, and show them their power. Then we shall learn how to apply it in our daily lives.

To be able to use what we call *Viveka* (discrimination), to learn how in every moment of our lives, in every one of our actions, to discriminate between what is right and wrong, true and false, we shall have to know the test of truth, which is purity, oneness. Everything that makes for oneness is truth. Love is truth, and hatred is false, because hatred makes for multiplicity. It is hatred that separates man from man; therefore it is wrong and false. It is a disintegrating power; it separates and destroys.

Love binds, love makes for that oneness. You become one, the mother with the child, families with the city, the whole world becomes one with the animals. For love is Existence, God Himself; and all this is the manifestation of that One Love, more or less expressed. The difference is only in degree, but it is the manifestation of that One Love throughout. Therefore in all our actions we have to judge whether it is making for diversity or for oneness. If for diversity we have to give it up, but if it makes for oneness we are sure it is good. So with our thoughts; we have to decide whether they make for disintegration, multiplicity, or for oneness, binding soul to soul and bringing one influence to bear. If they do this, we will take them up, and if not, we will throw them off as criminal.

The whole idea of ethics is that it does not depend on anything unknowable, it does not teach anything unknown, but in the language of the Upanishad, "The God whom you worship as an unknown God, the same I preach unto thee." It is through the Self that you know anything. I see the chair; but to see the chair, I have first to perceive myself and then the chair. It is in and through the Self that the chair is perceived. It is in and through the Self that you are known to me, that the whole world is known to me; and therefore to say this Self is unknown is sheer nonsense. Take off the Self and the whole universe vanishes. In and through the Self all knowledge comes...

These ideas of the ethics of Vedanta have to be worked out in detail. ...Do you feel for others? If you do, you are growing in oneness. If you do not feel for others, you may be the most intellectual giant ever born, but you will be nothing; you are but dry intellect, and you will remain so. And if you feel, even if you cannot read any book and do not know any language, you are in the right way....Feel like Christ and you will be a Christ; feel like Buddha and you will be a Buddha. It is feeling that is the life, the strength. ...It is one of the most practical things in Vedantic morality.[1]

The Vedantist says, the cause of all that is apparently evil is the limitation of the unlimited. The love, which gets limited into little channels and seems to be evil, eventually comes out at the other end and manifests itself as God. The Vedanta also says that the cause of all this apparent evil is in ourselves. Do not blame any supernatural being, neither be hopeless and despondent, nor think we are in a place from which we can never escape unless someone comes and lends us a helping hand. That cannot be, says the Vedanta. We are like silkworms; we make the thread out of our own substance and spin the cocoon, and, in course of time are imprisoned inside. But this is not forever...

What we are to understand is this, that what we call mistakes or evil, we commit because we are weak, and we are weak because we are ignorant. I prefer to call them mistakes. The word sin, although originally a very good word, has got a certain flavour about it that frightens me. Who makes us ignorant? We ourselves. We put our hands over our eyes and weep that it is dark. Take the hands away and there is light; the light exists always for us, the self-effulgent nature of the human soul. Do you not hear what your modern scientific men say? What is the cause of evolution? Desire. The animal wants to do something, but does not find the environment favourable, and, therefore, develops a new body. Who develops it? The animal itself, its will. You have developed from the lowest amoeba. Continue to exercise your will and it will take you higher still. The will is almighty. If it is almighty, you may say, why cannot I do everything? But you are thinking only of your little self. Look back on yourselves from the state of the amoeba to the human being; who made all that? Your own will. Can you deny then that it is almighty? That which has made you come up so high can make you go higher still. What you want is character, strengthening of the will.

If I teach you, therefore, that your nature is evil, that you should go home and sit in sackcloth and ashes and weep your lives out because you took certain false steps, it will not help you, but will weaken you all the more, and I shall be showing you the road to more evil than good. If this room is full of darkness for thousands of years and you come in and begin to weep and wail, "Oh the darkness", will the darkness vanish? Strike a match and light comes in a moment. What good will it do you to think all your lives, "Oh, I have done evil, I have made many mistakes"? It requires no ghost to tell us that. Bring in the light and the evil goes in a moment. Build up your character, and manifest your real nature, the Effulgent, the Resplendent, the Ever-Pure, and call It up in everyone that you see.[2]

The Ethical Idealism of Buddha

THE HISTORY OF THE WORLD shows that those who never thought of their little individuality were the greatest benefactors of the human race, and that the more men and women think of themselves, the less are they able to do for others. One is unselfishness, and the other selfishness. Clinging on to little enjoyments, and to desire the continuation and repetition of this state of things is utter selfishness. It arises not from any desire for truth, its genesis is not in kindness for other beings, but in the utter selfishness of the human heart, in the idea, "I will have everything, and do not care for anyone else." This is as it appears to me. I would like to see more moral men in the world like some of those grand old

The Ethical Idealism of Buddha

prophets and sages of ancient times who would have given up a hundred lives if they could by so doing benefit one little animal...

I would like to see moral men like Gautama Buddha, who did not believe in a Personal God or a personal soul, never asked about them, but was a perfect agnostic, and yet was ready to lay down his life for anyone, and worked all his life for the good of all, and thought only of the good of all. Well has it been said by his biographer, in describing his birth, that he was born for the good of the many, as a blessing to the many. He did not go to the forest to meditate for his own salvation; he felt that the world was burning, and that he must find a way out. "Why is there so much misery in the world?"—was the one question that dominated his whole life.[1]

It was the great Buddha, who never cared for the dualist gods, and who has been called an atheist and materialist, who yet was ready to give up his body for a poor goat. That Man set in motion the highest moral ideas any nation can have. Wherever there is a moral code, it is a ray of light from that Man. We cannot force the great hearts of the world into narrow limits, and keep them there, especially at this time in the history of humanity when there is a degree of intellectual development such as was never dreamed of even a hundred years ago, when a wave of scientific knowledge has arisen which nobody, even fifty years ago, would have dreamed of. By trying to force people into narrow limits you degrade them into animals and unthinking masses. You kill their moral life. What is now wanted is a combination of the greatest heart with the highest intellectuality, of infinite love with infinite knowledge. The Vedantist gives no other attributes to God except these three—that He is Infinite Existence, Infinite Knowledge, and Infinite Bliss, and he regards these three as One. Existence without knowledge and love cannot be; knowledge without love and love without knowledge cannot be. What we want is the harmony of Existence, Knowledge, and Bliss Infinite. For that is our goal. We want harmony, not one-sided development. And it is possible to have the intellect of a Shankara with the heart of a Buddha. I hope we shall all struggle to attain to that blessed combination.[2]

To help the suffering world was the gigantic task to which the Buddha gave prominence, brushing aside for the time being almost all other phases of religion; yet he had to spend years in self-searching to realise the great truth of the utter hollowness of clinging to a selfish individuality. A more unselfish and untiring worker is beyond our most sanguine imagination; yet who had harder struggles to realise the meaning of things than he? It holds good in all times that the greater the work, the more must have been the power of realisation behind. Working out the details of an already laid out masterly plan may not require much concentrated thought to back it, but the great impulses are only transformed great concentrations. The theory alone perhaps is sufficient for small exertions, but the push that creates the ripple is very different from the impulsion that raises the wave, and yet the ripple is only the embodiment of a bit of the power that generates the wave.[3]

He was the only man who was bereft of all motive power. There were other great men who all said, they were the Incarnations of God Himself, and that those who would believe in them would go to heaven. But what did Buddha say with his dying breath? "None can help you; help yourself; work out your own salvation." He said about himself, "Buddha is the name of infinite knowledge, infinite as the sky; I, Gautama, have reached that state; you will all reach that too if you struggle for it." Bereft of all motive power, he did not want to go to heaven, did not want money; he gave up his throne and everything else and went about begging his bread through the streets of India, preaching for the good of men and animals with a heart as wide as the ocean.

He was the only man who was ever ready to give up his life for animals, to stop a sacrifice. He once said to a king, "If the sacrifice of a lamb helps you to go to heaven, sacrificing a man will help you better; so sacrifice me." The king was astonished. And yet this man was without any motive power. He stands as the perfection of the active type, and the very height to which he attained shows that through the power of work we can also attain to the highest spirituality.

To many the path becomes easier if they believe in God. But the life of Buddha shows that even a man who does not believe in God, has no metaphysics, belongs to no sect, and does not go to any church, or temple, and is a confessed materialist, even he can attain to the highest. We have no right to judge him. I wish I had one infinitesimal part of Buddha's heart. Buddha may or may not have believed in God; that does not matter to me. He reached the same state of perfection to which others come by Bhakti—love of God—Yoga, or Jnana. Perfection does not come from belief or faith. Talk does not count for anything. Parrots can do that. Perfection comes through the disinterested performance of action.[4]

Let me tell you in conclusion a few words about one man who actually carried this teaching of *Karma-Yoga* into practice. That man is Buddha. He is the one man who ever carried this into perfect practice. All the prophets of the world, except Buddha, had

THE ETHICAL IDEALISM OF BUDDHA

external motives to move them to unselfish action. The prophets of the world, with this single exception, may be divided into two sets, one set holding that they are incarnations of God come down on earth, and the other holding that they are only messengers from God; and both draw their impetus for work from outside, expect reward from outside, however highly spiritual may be the language they use. But Buddha is the only prophet who said, "I do not care to know your various theories about God. What is the use of discussing all the subtle doctrines about the soul? Do good and be good. And this will take you to freedom and to whatever truth there is." He was, in the conduct of his life, absolutely without personal motives.

And what man worked more than he? Show me in history one character who has soared so high above all. The whole human race has produced but one such character, such high philosophy, such wide sympathy. This great philosopher, preaching the highest philosophy, yet had the deepest sympathy for the lowest of animals, and never put forth any claims for himself. He is the ideal *Karma-Yogi*, acting entirely without motive, and the history of humanity shows him to have been the greatest man ever born; beyond compare the greatest combination of heart and brain that ever existed, the greatest soul-power that has ever been manifested. He is the first great reformer the world has seen. He was the first who dared to say, "Believe not because some old manuscripts are produced, believe not because it is your national belief, because you have been made to believe it from your childhood; but reason it all out, and after you have analysed it, then, if you find that it will do good to one and all, believe it, live up to it, and help others to live up to it." He works best who works without any motive, neither for money, nor for fame, nor for anything else; and when a man can do that, he will be a Buddha, and out of him will come the power to work in such a manner as will transform the world. This man represents the very highest ideal of *Karma-Yoga*.[5]

Essential Moral Virtues

Mercy and Self-sacrifice

DO YOU ASK ANYTHING from your children in return for what you have given them? It is your duty to work for them, and there the matter ends. In whatever you do for a particular person, a city, or a state, assume the same attitude towards it as you have towards your children—expect nothing in return...

There are two things which guide the conduct of men: might and mercy. The exercise of might is invariably the exercise of selfishness. All men and women try to make the most of whatever power or advantage they have. Mercy is heaven itself; to be good, we have all to be merciful. Even justice and right should stand on mercy. All thought of obtaining return for the work we do hinders our spiritual progress; nay, in the end it brings misery. There is another way in which this idea of mercy and selfless charity can be put into practice; that is, by looking upon work as "worship" in case we believe in a Personal God...

This idea of complete self-sacrifice is illustrated in the following story: After the battle of Kurukshetra the five Pandava brothers performed a great sacrifice and made very large gifts to the poor. All people expressed amazement at the greatness and richness of the sacrifice, and said that such a sacrifice the world had never seen before. But, after the ceremony, there came a little mongoose, half of whose body was golden, and the other half brown; and he began to roll on the floor of the sacrificial hall. He said to those around, "You are all liars; this is no sacrifice." "What!" they exclaimed, "you say this is no sacrifice; do you not know how money and jewels were poured out to the poor and every one became rich and happy? This was the most wonderful sacrifice any man every performed."

But the mongoose said, "There was once a little village, and in it there dwelt a poor Brahmin with his wife, his son, and his son's wife. They were very poor and lived on small gifts made to them for preaching and teaching. There came in that land a three years' famine, and the poor Brahmin suffered

Essential Moral Virtues

more than ever. At last, when the family had starved for days, the father brought home one morning a little barley flour, which he had been fortunate enough to obtain, and he divided it into four parts, one for each member of the family. They prepared it for their meal, and just as they were about to eat, there was a knock at the door. The father opened it, and there stood a guest. Now in India a guest is a sacred person; he is as a god for the time being, and must be treated as such. So the poor Brahmin said, "Come in, sir; you are welcome." He set before the guest his own portion of the food, which the guest quickly ate and said, "Oh, sir, you have killed me; I have been starving for ten days, and this little bit has but increased my hunger." Then the wife said to her husband, "Give him my share," but the husband said, "Not so." The wife however insisted, saying, "Here is a poor man, and it is our duty as householders to see that he is fed, and it is my duty as a wife to give him my portion, seeing that you have no more to offer him." Then she gave her share to the guest, which he ate, and said he was still burning with hunger. So the son said, "Take my portion also; it is the duty of a son to help his father to fulfil his obligation." The guest ate that, but remained still unsatisfied; so the son's wife gave him her portion also. That was sufficient, and the guest departed, blessing them. That night those four people died of starvation. A few granules of that flour had fallen on the floor; and when I rolled my body on them, half of it became golden, as you see. Since then I have been travelling all over the world, hoping to find another sacrifice like that, but nowhere have I found one; nowhere else has the other half of my body been turned into gold. That is why I say this is no sacrifice."[1]

Service

Helping others physically by removing their physical needs, is indeed great, but the help is great according as the need is greater and according as the help is far-reaching. If a man's wants can be removed for an hour, it is helping him indeed; if his wants can be removed for a year, it will be more help to him; but if his wants can be removed for ever, it is surely the greatest help that can be given him.

Spiritual knowledge is the only thing that can destroy our miseries for ever; any other knowledge satisfies wants only for a time. It is only with the knowledge of the spirit that the faculty of want is annihilated for ever; so helping man spiritually is the highest help that can be given to him. He who gives man spiritual knowledge is the greatest benefactor of mankind and as such we always find that those were the most powerful of men who helped man in his spiritual needs, because spirituality is the true basis of all our activities in life. A spiritually strong and sound man will be strong in every other respect, if he so wishes. Until there is spiritual strength in man even physical needs cannot be well satisfied.

Next to spiritual comes intellectual help. The gift of knowledge is a far higher gift than that of food and clothes; it is even higher than giving life to a man, because the real life of man consists of knowledge. Ignorance is death, knowledge is life. Life is of very little value, if it is a life in the dark, groping through ignorance and misery. Next in order comes, of course, helping a man physically.

Therefore, in considering the question of helping others, we must always strive not to commit the mistake of thinking that physical help is the only help that can be given. It is not only the last but the least, because it cannot bring about permanent satisfaction. The misery that I feel when I am hungry is satisfied by eating, but hunger returns; my misery can cease only when I am satisfied beyond all want. Then hunger will not make me miserable; no distress, no sorrow will be able to move me. So, that help which tends to make us strong spiritually is the highest, next to it comes intellectual help, and after that physical help.

The miseries of the world cannot be cured by physical help only. Until man's nature changes, these physical needs will always arise, and miseries will always be felt, and no amount of physical help will cure them completely. The only solution of this problem is to make mankind pure. Ignorance is the mother of all the evil and all the misery we see. Let men have light, let them be pure and spiritually strong and educated, then alone will misery cease in the world, not before. We may convert every house in the country into a charity asylum, we may fill the land with hospitals, but the misery of man will still continue to exist until man's character changes.[2]

The great secret of true success, of true happiness, then, is this: the man who asks for no return, the perfectly unselfish man, is the most successful. It seems to be a paradox. Do we not know that every man who is unselfish in life gets cheated, gets hurt? Apparently, yes. "Christ was unselfish, and yet he was crucified." True, but we know that his unselfishness is the reason, the cause of a great victory—the crowning of millions upon millions of lives with the blessings of true success.

Ask nothing; want nothing in return. Give what you have to give; it will come back to you—but do not think of that now, it will come back multiplied a thousandfold—but the attention must not be on that.

Yet have the power to give: give, and there it ends. Learn that the whole of life is giving, that nature will force you to give. So, give willingly. Sooner or later you will have to give up. ...It is because we dare not give, because we are not resigned enough to accede to this grand demand of nature, that we are miserable. The forest is gone, but we get heat in return. The sun is taking up water from the ocean, to return it in showers. You are a machine for taking and giving: you take, in order to give.

Ask, therefore, nothing in return; but the more you give, the more will come to you. The quicker you can empty the air out of this room, the quicker it will be filled up by the external air; and if you close all the doors and every aperture, that which is within will remain, but that which is outside will never come in, and that which is within will stagnate, degenerate, and become poisoned. A river is continually emptying itself into the ocean and is continually filling up again. Bar not the exit into the ocean. The moment you do that, death seizes you.[3]

Duty

The *Bhagavad Gita* frequently alludes to duties dependent upon birth and position in life. Birth and position in life and in society largely determine the mental and moral attitude of individuals towards the various activities of life. It is therefore our duty to do that work which will exalt and ennoble us in accordance with the ideals and activities of the society in which we are born.[4]

The one point we ought to remember is that we should always try to see the duty of others through their own eyes, and never judge the customs of other peoples by our own standard. I am not the standard of the universe. I have to accommodate myself to the world, and not the world to me. So we see that environments change the nature of our duties, and doing the duty which is ours at any particular time is the best thing we can do in this world. Let us do that duty which is ours by birth; and when we have done that, let us do the duty which is ours by our position in life and in society. There is, however, one great danger in human nature, viz. that man never examines himself. He thinks he is quite as fit to be on the throne as the king. Even if he is, he must first show that he has done the duty of his own position; and then higher duties will come to him. When we begin to work earnestly in the world, nature gives us blows right and left and soon enables us to find out our position. No man can long occupy satisfactorily a position for which he is not fit. There is no use in grumbling against nature's adjustment. He who does the lower work is not therefore a lower man. No man is to be judged by the mere nature of his duties, but all should be judged by the manner and the spirit in which they perform them.[5]

It is the worker who is attached to results that grumbles about the nature of the duty which has fallen to his lot; to the unattached worker all duties are equally good, and form efficient instruments with which selfishness and sensuality may be killed, and the freedom of the soul secured. We are all apt to think too highly of ourselves. Our duties are determined by our deserts to a much larger extent than we are willing to grant. Competition rouses envy, and it kills the kindliness of the heart. To the grumbler all duties are distasteful; nothing will ever satisfy him, and his whole life is doomed to prove a failure. Let us work on, doing as we go whatever happens to be our duty, and being ever ready to put our shoulders to the wheel. Then surely shall we see the Light![6]

Duty is seldom sweet. It is only when love greases its wheels that it runs smoothly; it is a continuous friction otherwise. How else could parents do their duties to their children, husbands to their wives, and *vice versa*? Do we not meet with cases of friction every day in our lives? Duty is sweet only through love, and love shines in freedom alone. Yet is it freedom to be a slave to the senses, to anger, to jealousies and a hundred other petty things that must occur every day in human life? In all these little roughnesses that we meet with in life, the highest expression of freedom is to forbear.[7]

Our duty to others means helping others; doing good to the world. Why should we do good to the world? Apparently to help the world, but really to help ourselves. We should always try to help the world, that should be the highest motive in us; but if we consider well, we find that the world does not require our help at all. This world was not made that you or I should come and help it. I once read a sermon in which it was said, "All this beautiful world is very good, because it gives us time and opportunity to help others." Apparently, this is a very beautiful sentiment, but is it not a blasphemy to say that the world needs our help? We cannot deny that there is much misery in it; to go out and help others is, therefore, the best thing we can do, although in the long run, we shall find that helping others is only helping ourselves. ...The only help is that we get moral exercise. This world is neither good nor evil; each man manufactures a world for himself. If a blind man begins to think of the world, it is either as soft or hard, or as cold or hot. We are a mass of happiness or misery; we have seen that hundreds of times in our lives. As a rule, the young are optimistic and the old pessimistic. The young have life before them; the old complain their day is gone; hundreds of desires, which they cannot fulfil struggle in their hearts. Both are foolish nevertheless. Life is good or evil according to the state of mind in which we look at it, it is neither by itself. Fire, by itself, is neither good nor evil. When it keeps us warm we say, "How beautiful is fire!" When it burns our fingers, we blame it. Still, in itself it is neither good nor bad. According as we use it, it produces in us the feeling of good or bad; so also is this world. It is perfect. By perfection is meant that it is perfectly fitted to meet its ends. We may all be perfectly sure that it will go on beautifully well without us, and we need not bother our heads wishing to help it.

Yet we must do good; the desire to do good is the highest motive power we have, if we know all the time that it is a privilege to help others. Do not stand on a high pedestal and take five cents in your hand and say, "Here, my poor man," but be grateful that the poor man is there, so that by making a gift to him you are able to help yourself. It is not the receiver that is blessed, but it is the giver. Be thankful that you are allowed to exercise your power of benevolence and mercy in the world, and thus become pure and perfect.[8]

Chastity

Chastity is the first virtue in man or woman, and the man who, however he may have strayed away, cannot be brought to the right path by a gentle and loving and chaste wife is indeed very rare. The world is not yet as bad as that. ...What brutality is there which purity and chastity cannot conquer? A good, chaste wife, who thinks of every other man except her own husband as her child and has the attitude of a mother towards all men, will grow so great in the power of her purity that there cannot be a single man, however brutal, who will not breathe an atmosphere of holiness in her presence. Similarly, every husband must look upon all women, except his own wife, in the light of his own mother or daughter or sister. ...

The position of the mother is the highest in the world, as it is the one place in which to learn and exercise the greatest unselfishness. The love of God is the only love that is higher than a mother's love; all others are lower.[9]

Non-injury

Perfect morality is the all in all of complete control over mind. The man who is perfectly moral has nothing more to do; he is free. The man who is perfectly moral cannot possibly hurt anything or anybody. Non-injuring has to be attained by him who would be free. No one is more powerful than he who has attained perfect non-injuring. No one could fight, no one could quarrel, in his presence. Yes, his very presence, and nothing else, means peace, means love wherever he may be. Nobody could be angry or fight in his presence. Even the animals, ferocious animals, would be peaceful before him.[10]

Attention to Means

One of the greatest lessons I have learnt in my life is to pay as much attention to the means of work as to its end. ...I have been always learning great lessons from that one principle, and it appears to be that all the secret of success is there; to pay as much attention to the means as to the end.

Our great defect in life is that we are so much drawn to the ideal, the goal is so much more enchanting, so much more alluring, so much bigger in our mental horizon, that we lose sight of the details altogether.

But whenever failure comes, if we analyse it critically, in ninety-nine per cent of cases we shall find that it was because we did not pay attention to the means. Proper attention to the finishing, strengthening, of the means is what we need. With the means all right, the end must come. ...Once the ideal is chosen and the means determined, we may almost let go the ideal, because we are sure it will be there, when the means are perfected.[11]

Some Moral Precepts and Exhortations to Our Youths

THE FIRST GREAT THING to accomplish is to establish a character, to obtain, as we say, the *pratishthita prajna* (established Wisdom). This applies equally to individuals and to organised bodies of individuals.
...

Truth, purity, and unselfishness—wherever these are present, there is no power below or above the sun to crush the possessor thereof. Equipped with these, one individual is able to face the whole universe in opposition.[1]

Neither money pays, nor name, nor fame, nor learning; it is character that can cleave through adamantine walls of difficulties. Bear this in mind.[2]

Expansion is life, contraction is death. Love is life, and hatred is death. ...

Let us calmly and in a manly fashion go to work, instead of dissipating our energy in unnecessary frettings and fumings. I, for one, thoroughly believe that no power in the universe can withhold from anyone anything he really deserves. The past was great no doubt, but I sincerely believe that the future will be more glorious still.[3]

Renounce the lower so that you may get the higher. What is the foundation of society? Morality, ethics, laws. Renounce. Renounce all temptation to take your neighbour's property, to put hands upon your neighbour, all the pleasure of tyrannising over the weak, all the pleasure of cheating others by telling lies. Is not morality the foundation of society? What is marriage but the renunciation of unchastity? The savage does not marry. Man marries because he renounces. So on and on. Renounce! Renounce! Sacrifice! Give up! Not for zero. Not for nothing. But to get the higher.[4]

It is unswerving love and perfect unselfishness that conquer everything. We Vedantists, in every difficulty, ought to ask the subjective question: "Why do I see that?", "Why can I not conquer this with love?...

Great work requires great and persistent effort for a long time. Neither need we trouble ourselves if a few fail. It is in the nature of things that many should fall, that troubles should come, that tremendous difficulties should arise, that selfishness and all the other devils in the human heart should struggle hard when they are about to be driven out by the fire of spirituality. The road to the Good is the roughest and steepest in the universe. It is a wonder that so many succeed, no wonder that so many fall. Character has to be established through a thousand stumbles.[5]

In the *Katha Upanishad* the body is described as the chariot, the mind is the reins, the intellect is the charioteer, the senses are the horses, and the objects of the senses their road. The self is the rider, seated in the chariot. Unless the rider has understanding and can make the charioteer control his horses, he can never attain the goal; but the senses, like vicious steeds, will drag him where they please and may even destroy him.

These two currents are the great "check rein" in the hands of the charioteer, and he must get control of this to control the horses. We have to get the power to become moral; until we do that, we cannot control our actions. Yoga alone enables us to carry into practice the teachings of morality. To become moral is the object of Yoga.[6]

No force can be created; it can only be directed. Therefore we must learn to control the grand powers that are already in our hands and by will power make them spiritual instead of merely animal. Thus it is clearly seen that chastity is the corner-stone of all morality and of all religion.[7]

Be you holy and, above all, sincere; and do not for a moment give up your trust in the Lord, and you will see the light. Whatever is truth will remain for ever; whatever is not, none can preserve. We are helped in being born in a time when everything is quickly searched out. Whatever others think or do, lower not your standard of purity, morality, and love of God; above all, beware of all secret organisations. No one who loves God need fear any jugglery. Holiness is the highest and divinest power in earth and in heaven. "Truth alone triumphs, not untruth. Through truth alone is opened the way to God". Do not care for a moment who joins hands with you or not, be sure that you touch the hand of the Lord. That is enough.[8]

The diabolical man is a part of my body as a wound or a burn is. We have to nurse it and get it better; so continually nurse and help the diabolical man, until he "heals" and is once more happy and healthy.[9]

And above all, one thing is necessary. Ay, for ages we have been saturated with awful jealousy; we are always getting jealous of each other. Why has this man a little precedence, and not I? Even in the worship of God we want precedence, to such a state of slavery have we come. This is to be avoided. If there is any crying sin in India at this time it is this slavery. Every one wants to command, and no one wants to obey; and this is owing to the absence of that wonderful *Brahmacharya* system of yore. First, learn to obey. The command will come by itself. Always first learn to be a servant and then you will be fit to be a master. Avoid this jealousy, and you will do great works that have yet to be done. Our ancestors did most wonderful works, and we look back upon their work with veneration and pride. But we also are going to do great deeds, and let others look back with blessings and pride upon us as their ancestors.[10]

What we want is strength, so believe in yourselves. We have become weak, and that is why occultism and mysticism come to us—these creepy things; there may be great truths in them, but they have nearly destroyed us. Make your nerves strong. What we want is muscles of iron and nerves of steel. We have wept long enough. No more weeping, but stand on your feet and be men. It is a man-making religion that we want. It is man-making theories that we want. It is man-making education all round that we want. And here is the test of truth—anything that makes you weak physically, intellectually, and spiritually, reject as poison; there is no life in it, it cannot be true. Truth is strengthening. Truth is purity, truth is all-knowledge; truth must be strengthening, must be enlightening, must be invigorating.[11]

Nothing else is necessary but these—*love, sincerity,* and *patience.* What is life but growth, i.e. expansion, i.e. love? Therefore all love is life; it is the only law of life; all selfishness is death, and this is true here or hereafter. It is life to do good, it is death not to do good to others. Feel, my children, feel; feel for the poor, the ignorant, the downtrodden; feel till the heart stops and the brain reels and you think you will go mad—then pour the soul out at the feet of the Lord, and then will come power, help, and indomitable energy. Struggle, struggle, was my motto for the last ten years. Struggle, still say I. When it was all dark, I used to say, struggle; when light is breaking in, I still say, struggle. Be not afraid, my children.[12]

Three things are necessary to make every man great, every nation great:
- Conviction of the powers of goodness.
- Absence of jealousy and suspicion.
- Helping all who are trying to be and do good.[13]

SOME MORAL PRECEPTS AND EXHORTATIONS...   *109*

Gird up your loins, my boy. ...Well, my boy, this is the school of misery, which is also the school for great souls and prophets for the cultivation of sympathy, of patience, and, above all, of an indomitable iron will which quakes not even if the universe be pulverised at our feet.[14]

"Ours not to reason why, ours but to do and die." Be of good cheer and believe that we are selected by the Lord to do great things, and we will do them. Hold yourself in readiness, i.e. be pure and holy, and love for love's sake. Love the poor, the miserable, the down-trodden, and the Lord will bless you.[15]

Fight on bravely! Life is short. Give it up to a great cause.[16]

Love immense and infinite, broad as the sky and deep as the ocean—this is the one great gain in life. Blessed is he who gets it.[17]

If, in this hell of a world, one can bring a little joy and peace even for a day into the heart of a single person, that much alone is true. This I have learnt after suffering all my life; all else is mere moonshine.[18]

Don't be ruffled if now and then you get a brush from the world; it will be over in no time, and everything will be all right.[19]

Be moral. Be brave. Be a heart-whole man. Strictly moral, brave unto desperation. Don't bother your head with religious theories. Cowards only sin, brave men never, no, not even in mind. Try to love anybody and everybody. Be a *man* and try to make those immediately under your care....brave, moral, and sympathising. No religion for you, my children, but morality and bravery. No cowardice, no sin, no crime, no weakness—the rest will come of itself.[20]

Think, all of you, that you are the infinitely powerful Atman, and see what strength comes out... . Self-depreciation! What is it for? I am the child of the Infinite, the all-powerful Divine Mother. What means disease, or fear, or want to me? Stamp out the negative spirit as if it were a pestilence, and it will conduce to your welfare in every way. No negative, all positive, affirmative. I *am* , God *is* , everything is in me. I *will* manifest health, purity, knowledge, whatever I want. ..."Thou art Energy, impart energy unto me. Thou art Strength, impart strength unto me. Thou art Spirituality, impart spirituality unto me. Thou art Fortitude, impart fortitude unto me!"

One must think of oneself as strong and invulnerable.[21]

We want some disciples—fiery young men—do you see?—intelligent and brave, who dare to go to the jaws of Death, and are ready to swim the ocean across. ...We want hundreds like that, both men and women.[22]

What work do you expect from men of little hearts?—Nothing in the world! You must have an iron will if you would cross the ocean. You must be strong enough to pierce mountains.[23]

The success of your undertakings depends wholly upon your mutual love. There is no good in store so long as malice and jealousy and egotism will prevail. ...Know that talking ill of others in private is a sin. You must wholly avoid it. Many things may occur to the mind, but it gradually makes a mountain of a molehill if you try to express them. Everything is ended if you forgive and forget....Shyness won't do any more....He who has infinite patience and infinite energy at his back, will alone succeed.[24]

Come? Do something heroic! Brother, what if you do not attain *Mukti*, what if you suffer damnation a few times? Is the saying untrue:

> *Manasi vacasi kāye puṇyapīyūṣapūrṇāḥ,*
> *tribhuvanam upakāraśreṇibhiḥ prīṇayantaḥ;*
> *Paraguṇaparamāṇum parvatīkritya nityam,*
> *nijahridi vikasantaḥ santi santaḥ kiyantaḥ—*

"There are some saints, who, full of holiness in thought, word, and deed, please the whole world by their numerous beneficent acts, and who develop their own hearts by magnifying an atom of virtue in others as if it were as great as a mountain" (Bhartrihari, *Nitishataka*).[25]

Can anything be done unless everybody exerts himself to his utmost? *Udyoginām puruṣa simham upaiti lakshmīḥ*. "It is the man of action, the lion-heart, that the Goddess of Wealth resorts to." No need of looking behind. FORWARD! We want infinite energy, infinite zeal, infinite courage, and infinite patience, then only will great things be achieved.[26]

Follow truth wherever it may lead you; carry ideas to their utmost logical conclusions. Do not be cowardly and hypocritical.[27]

Be bold! My children should be brave, above all. ...Preach the highest truths broadcast. Do not fear losing your respect or causing unhappy friction. Rest assured that if you serve truth in spite of temptations to forsake it, you will attain a heavenly strength in the face of which men will quail to speak before you things which you do not believe to be true. People will be convinced of what you will say to them if you can strictly serve truth for fourteen years continually, without swerving from it. Thus you will confer the greatest blessing on the masses, unshackle their bondages, and uplift the whole nation.[28]

Him I call a *Mahātman* (great soul) whose heart bleeds for the poor, otherwise he is a *Durātman* (wicked soul).[29]

Some Moral Precepts and Exhortations... 113

So long as the millions live in hunger and ignorance, I hold every man a traitor who, having been educated at their expense, pays not the least heed to them![30]

Go, all of you, wherever there is an outbreak of plague or famine, or wherever the people are in distress, and mitigate their sufferings. At the most you may die in the attempt. What of that? How many like you are being born and dying like worms every day? What difference does that make to the world at large? Die you must, but have a great ideal to die for, and it is better to die with a great ideal in life.[31]

You have now to make the character of Mahāvira your ideal. See how at the command of Rāmachandra he crossed the ocean. He had no care for life or death! He was a perfect master of his senses and wonderfully sagacious. You have now to build your life on this great ideal of personal service. Through that, all other ideals will gradually manifest in life. Obedience to the Guru without questioning, and strict observance of *Brahmacharya*—this is the secret of success. As on the one hand Hanumān represents the ideal of service, so on the other hand he represents leonine courage, striking the whole world with awe.[32]

Even the greatest fool can accomplish a task if it be after his heart. But the intelligent man is he who can convert every work into one that suits his taste.[33]

As I grow older I find that I look more and more for greatness in little things. I want to know what a great man eats and wears, and how he speaks to his servants. I want to find a Sir Philip Sidney greatness. Few men would remember the thirst of others, even in the moment of death. But anyone will be great in a great position. Even the coward will grow brave in the glare of the footlights. The world looks on. Whose hearts will not throb? Whose pulse will not quicken till he can do his best? More and more, the true greatness seems to me that of the worm, doing its duty silently, steadily, from moment to moment, and hour to hour.[34]

We must have life-building, man-making, character-making assimilation of ideas. If you have assimilated five ideas and made them your life and character, you have more education than any man who has got by heart a whole library.[35]

To me the very essence of education is concentration of mind, not the collecting of facts. If I had to do my education over again, and had any voice in the matter, I would not study facts at all. I would develop the power of concentration and detachment, and then with a perfect instrument I could collect facts at will.[36]

What is education? Is it book-learning? No. Is it diverse knowledge? Not even that. The training by which the current and expression of will are brought under control and become fruitful is called education.[37]

Why did not Christ say in the Sermon on the Mount, "Blessed are they that are always cheerful and always hopeful for they have already the kingdom of heaven"? I am sure, He must have said it, He with the sorrows of a whole world in His heart, He who likened the saintly soul with the child—but it was not noted down.[38]

In the Western world the idea of a religious man is that he never smiles, that a dark cloud must always hang over his face, which, again, must be long-drawn with the jaws almost collapsed. People with emaciated bodies and long faces are fit subjects for the physician, they are not *Yogis*. It is the cheerful mind that is persevering. It is the strong mind that hews its way through a thousand difficulties.[39]

The strong, the well-knit, the young, the healthy, the daring alone are fit to be *Yogis*. To the *Yogi* everything is bliss, every human face that he sees brings cheerfulness to him. That is the sign of a virtuous man. Misery is caused by sin, and by no other cause. What business have you with clouded faces? It is terrible. If you have a clouded face, do not go out that day, shut yourself up in your room. What right have you to carry this disease out into the world?

When your mind has become controlled, you have control over the whole body; instead of being a slave to this machine, the machine is your slave. Instead of this machine being able to drag the soul down, it becomes its greatest helpmate.[40]

"This Atman is first to be heard of." Hear day and night that you are that Soul. Repeat it to yourselves day and night till it enters into your very veins, till it tingles in every drop of blood, till it is in your flesh and bone. Let the whole body be full of that one ideal, "I am the birthless, the deathless, the blissful, the omniscient, the omnipotent, ever-glorious Soul." Think on it day and night; think on it till it becomes part and parcel of your life. Meditate upon it, and out of that will come work.

"Out of the fullness of the heart the mouth speaketh," and out of the fullness of the heart the hand worketh also. Action will come. Fill yourselves with the idea; whatever you do, think well on it. All your actions will be magnified, transformed, deified, by the very power of the thought. If matter is powerful, thought is omnipotent. Bring this thought to bear upon your life, fill yourselves with the thought of your almightiness, your majesty, and your glory.[41]

Seek not, touch not with your toes even, anything that is uncanny. Let your souls ascend day and night like an "unbroken string" unto the feet of the Beloved whose throne is in your own hearts and let the rest take care of themselves, that is the body and everything else. Life is evanescent, a fleeting dream; youth and beauty fade. Say day and night, "Thou art my father, my mother, my husband, my love, my lord, my God—I want nothing but Thee, nothing but Thee, nothing but Thee. Thou in me, I in Thee, I am Thee. Thou art me."...

Do not go for glass beads leaving the mine of diamonds! This life is a great chance. What, seekest thou the pleasures of the world?—He is the fountain of all bliss. Seek for the highest, aim at that highest, and you *shall* reach the highest.[42]

REFERENCES

[CW below refers to *The Complete Works of Swami Vivekananda*, Advaita Ashrama, Kolkata; LSV refers to *Life of Swami Vivekananda* by His Eastern and Western Disciples; the Roman numerals and the Arabic numerals following CW and LSV refer to the volume number and to the page numbers respectively.]

Ethics and Morality: The Real Basis of Life

1. CW, v, 192-93.

Love and Renunciation: The Motive Power of the Universe

1. CW, ii, 173. 2. CW, ii, 353-54.

The Philosophic Background

1. CW, ii, 355. 2. CW, i, 389-90.
3. CW, i, 430-36.

The Rationale of Ethics

1. CW, iii, 189. 2. CW, vi, 5-6.
3. CW, i, 364-65. 4. CW, ii, 80-83.
5. CW, i, 181-82.

Self-abnegation: The Basis of Moral Life

1. CW, ii, 62-64.
2. CW, i, 80.
3. CW, i, 85-86.
4. CW, viii, 146-47.
5. CW, vii, 102.
6. CW, iii, 129-30.

Morality Not an End in Itself: Freedom Its Goal

1. CW, v, 282.
2. CW, i, 108-10.

Morality: Its Relative Aspects

1. CW, vi, 109.
2. CW, i, 36-37 and 41-42.

Morality: Its Absolute Standard

1. CW, i, 110-11.

Utility of Morality and Ethics

1. CW, ii, 83-84.
2. CW, ii, 97-99.

Ethics: The Way and the Method

1. CW, ii, 33-35.
2. CW, i, 171-73.
3. CW, ii, 137.

Action and Its Effect on Character

1. CW, i, 27-35.
2. CW, i, 53-55.
3. CW, i, 207-08.

Ethical Principles and Practical Life

1. CW, ii, 292-307.
2. CW, ii, 355-57.

The Ethical Idealism of Buddha

1. CW, ii, 351-52.
2. CW, ii, 143.
3. CW, iv, 283.
4. CW, iv, 136-37.
5. CW, i, 116-18.

Essential Moral Virtues

1. CW, i, 59-61.
2. CW, i, 52-53.
3. CW, ii, 4-6.
4. CW, i, 64
5. CW, i, 65-66.
6. CW, i, 71.
7. CW, i, 67.
8. CW, i, 75-76.
9. CW, i, 67-68.
10. CW, vi, 126
11. CW, ii, 1.

Some Moral Precepts and Exhortations to Our Youths

1. CW, iv, 278-79.
2. CW, vii, 487.
3. CW, iv, 366.
4. CW, iv, 243.
5. CW, viii, 383.
6. CW, viii, 43.
7. CW, viii, 46.
8. CW, viii, 381-82.
9. CW, vii,103.
10. CW, iii, 134-35.
11. CW, iii, 224-25.
12. CW, iv, 367.
13. CW, viii, 299.
14. CW, v, 15-16.
15. CW, v, 23.
16. CW, v, 37.
17. CW, v, 144.
18. CW, v, 177.
19. CW, vi, 245.
20. CW, v, 3.
21. CW, vi, 276-77.
22. CW, vi, 292.
23. CW, vi, 297.
24. CW, vi, 304-05.
25. CW, vi, 314-15.
26. CW, vi, 383-84.
27. CW, vi, 121.
28. CW, v, 264-65.
29. CW, v, 58.
30. CW, v, 58.
31. CW, v, 383-84.
32. CW, vii, 232.
33. CW, vii, 508.
34. L.S.V, ii, 471.
35. CW, iii, 302.
36. CW, vi, 38-39.
37. CW, iv, 490.
38. CW, vi, 374.
39. CW, iii, 69.
40. CW, i, 264-65.
41. CW, ii, 302.
42. CW, vi, 262.